# One
## Whatever the cost

# One Goal
# Whatever the cost

Gillian March

New Wine Press

New Wine Press
an imprint of
RoperPenberthy Publishing Ltd
Springfield House
23 Oatlands Drive
Weybridge
Surrey KT13 9LZ
UK

ISBN 978-1-903905-76-0

Typeset by Avocet Typeset, Chilton, Aylesbury, Bucks
Cover design by Steve Coleman
Printed in the UK

*Through sunshine, rain and clouds You've led,*

*Through deepest sea, up steepest hill*

*A mantle of protection spread*

*About my path with wondrous skill.*

*So keep me true, though tears be shed*

*Desiring that Your will fulfil*

*I press towards the way ahead*

*Where lies one goal to aim at still.*

'Does commitment to Christ make a difference? If in doubt, read this book. Gillian left her privileged, aristocratic backgound to minister to the neediest in society. Her account of Christ's transformation of a prostitute, or a prisoner on hunger strike, or a crowd of drug addicts makes compulsive reading. Gillian's book will be an inspiration to you.'

*Canon Michael Green*

# Foreword

by members of my last church

I got to know Gillian in the 80's when she came to our church as incumbent's wife. As they and the church encountered various challenges, I witnessed Gillian first-hand at intercession. I saw in her a rare tenacity in clinging to the hem of the Lord's robes and not letting go. I also had the privilege of sitting under her preaching ministry. She was always well prepared, saturating herself in the Scriptures and longing to unfold the mind and purpose of God to her hearers. There was and is no compromise in Gillian. In preaching as well as in praying, she is totally rooted in Scripture, open to the Holy Spirit's leading and deeply passionate to see the Lord Jesus glorified. It is a reflection of how she lives her life; one hundred per cent committed to the cause of Christ's kingdom.

*Mary Sayer* (churchwarden's wife)

Gillian had a prophetic ministry and put the telling of that message above any thoughts of popularity or friendship. As with the prophets of old, Gillian was hated by some, but loved by others, but praise God they heard His necessary message. I was one who loved my dear sister, and through her message was blessed. Gillian was also used by the Lord to heal people. One such person was Ivy, the church cleaner, but who was not a church goer. She hobbled up to the vicarage front door to say she was resigning because her twisted feet were giving her such pain, due to arthritis. She loves to tell the story of how 'Gillian fell to her knees and started praying. My feet were made new, like babies feet, so at last I could wear shoes instead of slippers!' Needless to say, Ivy continued the cleaning job, became a member of a city church and also helps to serve and clear the tables, now in her eighties. Gillian had introduced her to a powerful Saviour.

*Steve Myall* (preacher)

Gillian is a brave courageous Christian, sold out for the Lord. She loves to tell people about Jesus and to teach those who are young in the faith how to know Him better. She was fantastic in a crisis and generous with her time. She would pray for you unstintingly and constantly – a real prayer warrior. She is talented and discerning and has read much Christian literature. She can be challenging, wielding the sword of the spirit as a valiant disciple, despite suffering pain and having long periods of ill health for many years. She longed for us to grow in greater maturity. She considered it enormously important to put in place a foundation and this caused me to grow into the Christian I am today. This is the sort of legacy we all hope we shall leave behind. There will be gems in this book.

*Trish Stevens* (vicar's secretary)

# Acknowledgements

I want to thank all my family and friends for their continual encouragement. I am so grateful to my daughter, Rachel, for her wonderful help in typing up and editing this book, to Sylvia Mandeville for the sacrificial time she has given and the excellent advice, to Jonathan Harley who inspired me to get started when my dream to write this book had waned and to my husband Tony, who has been the most enormous support and has always been so patient with me. My greatest thanks is to my Lord and Saviour, Jesus Christ, who gave His life for me and then gave His life to me when I was nearly twenty one years old. He has been transforming me gradually ever since, though I still have a very long way to go. I have told my story, some in prose and some in poetry, without hiding my trials, triumphs, failures and disasters. I have tried to be absolutely honest and real and I pray this book will bless each reader. Some names and places have been changed to protect identity (these are where the surname or place name has been omitted.)

*Gillian March*
December 2012

# Contents

# Contents

# Roots explored

"Listen my daughter, consider and give ear. Forget your people and your father's house, for the King is enthralled with your beauty. He is now your Lord. Worship only Him." Psalm 45:10 and 11

When I was twelve years old I went to visit my maternal grandfather, William Holland. I remember him opening a large book and showing me where he was in the royal tree. Recently, I read his sister's book about her grandfather, Tristram Holland who was a canon of Durham cathedral in the nineteenth century. He was the most famous ornithologist of his generation whom many sought out and visited. These included Jung, Freud, Darwin, the Duke of Wellington and the future King and Queen, just to mention a few. Thus I had a somewhat aristocratic background, yet with only the trappings of a distant lifestyle, because my father was a clergyman on a meagre income.

My grandfather at the time when I went to visit him was the vicar of St. Mary Woolnoth in the city of London. He was also the Lord Mayor's chaplain. If the Lord Mayor failed to pay the ground rent of the mansion house to the vicar incumbent of St. Mary's, the mansion house would have become the property of my grandfather! As the Lord Mayor's chaplain, he was invited by the Queen to Buckingham Palace for lunch and asked to say grace. He felt embarrassed, because he missed out the middle and said; "Thank you Heavenly Father ... for the Lord Jesus Christ." I think that to be the best grace ever! However, for many years before this my grandfather had been a missionary in India with The Church Missionary Society. He became the principal of St John's Agra and then St Paul's Calcutta. He developed a friendship with Gandhi, who once told him; "If Christians were more like Christ, I would become one" – a very sad reflection on the church.

My grandfather, while a curate in the north of England, became engaged to my grandmother when she was still at school and only sixteen. For this disgrace she was expelled! They married seven years later and had two girls in India. The elder, my mother Grace, was only just one year old when her sister Muriel was born. Due to lack of hygiene, my grandmother developed a fever and died within a week. The little girls were almost immediately shipped to Langholm in Scotland, where their grandfather lived in a large imposing mansion set in a very large and beautiful estate called Broomholm, next to that of Sir Alec Douglas Hume's family estate. Their grandfather was a vicar too, and also the local Laird. They enjoyed what might be described as an idyllic lifestyle. Cars were not yet in vogue, and the various trips were made by pony and trap. There were six servants and a nanny. Family prayers were held in the drawing room, with the family sitting in armchairs and the servants on benches. This rankled with my mother. As they grew up, the children joined in with trout and salmon fishing in their own estate, grouse shooting, tennis parties and all the usual social activities.

My mother's grandparents name was Maxwell, and I read in a newspaper article recently, 'The Maxwell's have been known in Langholm and Eskdale for upwards of three centuries. The founder was Ewen de Malcuswell, who accompanied King Malcolm III at the siege of Alnwick in 1093. This Baron married a daughter of the Lord of Galloway, and afterwards received the custody of Caelaverock castle. The first Maxwell was Herbert, son of Sir Emer Maxwell, Sheriff of Dumfries, who received from Sir William de Kunyberg the grant of the Laird in the Barony of Staplegordon. It was in this old church yard of the Barony that the mausoleum of the Maxwell's is situated.

It was a Maxwell who was appointed Warden of the Marches in 1425, and in 1488, John, the fourth Lord Maxwell, not only held this office, but was also the Lord of the regality of Eskdale. When fighting for King James IV John Maxwell was killed at Flodden, and it was to his son, the fifth Lord Maxwell, that the interest of Langholm and Eskdale chiefly attaches. Broomholm comes into the Maxwell-Eskdale history in the fourteenth century and since this time, the property and estate has always been associated with this famous border family.'

Both my mother and her sister were sent to boarding schools; my mother to Sherborne Ladies College and her sister to Casterton. They only saw their father once every five years, when he was home on furlough. Thus they were virtually orphans, and the seeds of this had a profound effect on my mother's life. When my mother left school, because she was completely undomesticated, she went to a domestic science college in London. The purpose was to become capable of looking after her middle aged bereaved father in India, and to get to know him. When she arrived in India, she excitedly told him of her ambition, and his reply literally slew her. He said, "I am now engaged to the niece of Lord Caldicott," who was then the Lord Chancellor, Sir Thomas Inskip "and I don't need you." From that day onwards my mother suffered with sleeplessness. If she had received the support of prayer and counselling, how different this might have been.

My mother Grace and my father John Marcon met in Lovedale in the Nilgiri Hills of India, while my father was a short term missionary with the Society for the Propagation of the Gospel. They got engaged at the foot of Mount Everest and then returned to England. My father went to Cuddesdon Theological College in Oxford, and my mother went to train at the Radcliffe Infirmary as a nurse. My father had been an undergraduate at Oriel College Oxford, where his forebears had always gone, and hence there is a hall named after them, called Marcon hall, my maiden name. My father excelled at tennis and got into the Oxford team. Unfortunately, one fateful weekend he decided to go home, unaware of the Oxbridge match, and so he missed his blue.

My father was also a keen lepidopterist, and all our childhood he spent hours catching *Vars* (short for variation butterflies), particularly on the South Downs, often taking one of his children with him. Then in the evenings, he would set these precious creatures with incredible skill and patience. In fact he gathered a huge priceless collection which he eventually sold because he felt his hobby was becoming an idol. By this time he had already become the leading lepidopterist of the twentieth century particularly in the variety 'Blues' and his butterflies are now in the Natural History Museum in London. These were surely different days. It is hard to imagine today's clergy having time for such a demanding hobby.

My father went to Charterhouse public school where he started his butterfly collection. He became one of the 'fives' pair for the school, a game similar to squash, but played with the hands. He was taught French by the famous Mallory, who later climbed Mount Everest with Irving, reached the summit, but sadly died on the descent and whose body has recently been found. My father hated school, though I guess these interests were a useful distraction.

When my father was an old man, the Carthusian Society asked him to be the speaker at an annual re-union and of course he spoke on butterflies. The BBC heard of this and invited him to speak on radio. All the family listened with rapt attention, and amongst his many guffaws, for he had a huge laugh, we could hardly hear him tell the story of trying to catch a butterfly in the war while a Doodlebug was right overhead. He thought nothing of this, and was only intent on gaining his prize catch, which he could always see from over a hundred yards away. With incredible stealth and slickness of hand, he would pop the net over this poor creature and put it into a glass lidded box ready for chloroforming in the evening.

My father was also a keen skater and a real character, as you might already have gathered. He often took me to the Crumbles at Eastbourne, or Hailsham pond or Brighton ice rink. One particular winter when there was much snow, he built an ice rink on the vicarage lawn by banking up the snow into a kind of large cake, and then hosing it down until it froze. One Sunday he returned from the morning service still clad in his cassock and skated on his ice rink. The Bishop happened to call unexpectedly and caught him at it. "What do you think you are doing, Marcon?" the Bishop scolded! Although my father taught me to skate, I could never dance like he did.

This is only a rough sketch of my family background, but it will give you some idea of my roots. When I was nearly twenty one years old, I met the King of Kings, the Lord Jesus Christ, and I gave my life to Him – unreservedly. This story I will relate later. Just after this, I was invited to become a debutante and be presented to the Queen. Lady Margaret Elphinstone was then a Lady in waiting to the Queen and I think we were vaguely related to her. Somehow I had no inclination to accept the offer, for my whole life had now gone into a totally different direction. I had no interest in society life anymore.

Much later my mother gave me her signet ring with the Holland crest engraved on it, which Harry Collins of Tunbridge Wells, now the crown jeweller, saw me wearing and specially commented on. Unfortunately soon afterwards I lost this ring in our garden. It happened that the Queen of Sweden's brother in law came to lunch with us, and I mentioned that I had lost my signet ring. He enquired about the coat of arms on the seal and when I replied "the Lion and the Unicorn," he exclaimed, "do you realise this is a royal crest." I then felt very sad that I had lost this priceless part of my heritage.

Nevertheless, I decided to check with Harry Collins and the York Herald at the College of Arms to make absolutely certain this was indeed the royal crest. I was assured that this was so and informed that the crest came into being with King James I. Between them they agreed to make a template for the crest and then remake the ring with the lion and the unicorn engraved. Even our insurance company agreed to foot the bill.

However, as I was reading my scripture portion for the day soon after this, I stumbled on Psalm 45: "Forget your family and your father's house. Listen carefully to me and incline your ear. The King is now your Lord. Worship only Him!" The Lord was clearly showing me that I had to leave behind my ancestry and any link with the earthly royal family, albeit tenuous, for I was now in His Holy family. I knew then that I had to relinquish any pride I took in my heredity if I was to obey the Lord and receive His far greater heavenly blessings.

"God forbid that I should glory, save in the cross of our Lord Jesus Christ, by whom the world is crucified to me and I to the world." Gal 6.14

## New Family

*O listen my daughter, I'm beckoning to you,*
*Consider my fair one and incline your ear.*
*Forget now your family; this you must do,*
*And come to Me only, my daughter so dear.*

*Now loosen your ties with your father's old home.*
*Pursue the great King who alone is your Lord;*
*Just leave behind ancestry. Come where you're known.*
*Yes, come to my palace, My mercy record.*

*Now enter with gladness and joy in your heart,*
*And see all the glories bequeathed by My hand.*
*Come, flee your old lifestyle, from this now depart,*
*And worship Me only; with Me you must stand.*

*O realise your beauty is lovely to Me.*
*The beauty of righteousness I have bestowed.*
*Thank me for this treasure within that I see.*
*Praise Me for this blessing – My love to you showed.*

Psalm 45; 10–16

# Childhood memories

"He shall turn the hearts of the fathers to their children, and the hearts of the children to their fathers."
Malachi 4.6

Surrounded by little monotonous houses one side, typical seaside dwellings on another, a church school at the bottom of a garden, a recreation ground opposite and nearby roads which were so narrow that the owners slung their washing lines from one side to the other, was a tall flint stone wall. This wall surrounded a very large garden in which stood an imposing house, a vicarage, and it was my home for nearly twenty years. We therefore led a secluded lifestyle, very different from those who lived around us. It seems incongruous today, but things were different eighty years ago.

We had several servants; there was a residential maid, a char lady and a gardener. When we were born, my mother always employed a nurse for the first six weeks, then a nanny and then a governess until we were five years old. The maid, called Jude and her son Reg, lived in the cellar in which were eleven rooms used for all sorts of purposes. This included a laundry and a work shop for my father to make and mend things in a 'Heath Robinson' fashion. There was electricity but no heating and so the cellar was very damp. The parish nurse lived upstairs with us. I have a brother called Dick, who is sixteen months older than I and a sister, called Susan who is five years younger. Thus we were nine altogether living in our home.

The garden held many delights for children. There was a lawn on which either badminton or more usually croquet was set up, and lots of large shrubs and trees to climb and in which to play hide and seek. There was an orchard full of apple and pear trees of many varieties and also a cherry, almond and huge fig tree. The kitchen garden was filled with every kind of fruit and vegetable imaginable. A peach tree spread out on a wall beside the greenhouse, in which my father grew tomatoes and potted up plants. There was also a large field, part of which was used for a garage and the rest rented out as an allotment. There was a chicken run, a butterfly cage the size of a box room, two garden sheds and a summer house with a flat roof. Beside this, a tree conveniently grew so that we could clamber up it and make ourselves our own little house on the top.

Each of us children had our own bedroom, mine being the largest and the best and in which we took great pride. In fact our bedrooms virtually became our own sitting rooms. There we would entertain a member of the family with a special tea party and in the winter be allowed to light a coal fire in the grate. We always tried to outdo each other in excellence. After every lunch we had to be as quiet as mice so that our parents could have an hour's sleep, after which mother would play board games or cards with us. Meal times were leisurely and full of erudite conversation which should have furnished me with a good general knowledge, had it not been for my dreaminess and lack of attention. My brother and I both loved playing the piano, which irritated my father when he was preparing sermons. My sister joined us in our love of acting. So we had concerts and plays to which all adults were expected to attend and duly applaud, however we performed!

Christmas dinner was always very special with a grand variety of luxurious foods, when the old fashioned finger bowls would appear on the table. At the end of the meal there would be toasts and then everyone would be expected to give a speech, at which Dick excelled, this being his forte. Although we tried, Susan and I virtually said nothing, for neither of us were capable at this stage of our lives. After the meal, all of us would go out and play hockey on the lawn. We might have had two or three hockey sticks between us so that most of us used whatever we could find, such as brooms, mops or any other contrivances. The purpose was to shake down the large dinner and, of course, to have fun. It would have been hilarious had anyone watched.

## Christmas

*It's Christmas Eve, and stars above shine bright.*
*White snow lies thick upon the frozen ground.*
*The world is fast asleep and out of sight.*
*The silence broken only by the sound*
*Of owls heard hooting to themselves in flight,*
*With some poor creature in their claws, they've found.*

*The fire in hearth still flickering, nearly out.*
*The Christmas tree all decked with twinkling light*
*And presents piled around; there is no doubt*
*Will bring excited voices of delight*
*When morning comes, and happy children shout*
*For joy; the great day's come. Past the long night.*

*Now sweet aromas from the kitchen rise.*
*The turkey safely in the oven roasts.*
*All hands on deck, awaiting great surprise.*
*For Christmas dinner, though traditional, boasts*
*Each single year new special enterprise,*
*Of course applauded with appropriate toasts.*

*Significance is lost for this event*
*By most of us; few realise or lend*
*A thought to this stupendous day; resent*
*An interruption to their mirth, to spend*
*A minute thinking what it really meant*
*For God, from heav'n to earth, His Son to send.*

*Some see the stable and the manger rough,*
*Perhaps in tableaux vivants at a school*
*And think how sweet and beautiful, not tough*
*As it most surely was. But man's a fool*
*When comprehending holy things; enough*
*We've comfort — yet for God another rule!*

*It may be that they sing the well-known song*
*Of Christmas; those old carols penned in rhyme.*
*May even think to join the church's throng*
*And love the mellow sound from church bell's chime.*
*May hear the Holy Scriptures, yet not long*
*To know the Saviour, born at Christmas time.*

*For hearts are hardened by the evil one.*
*Of all the days within the calendar*
*They're only drawn to pleasure and to fun.*
*There's so much this miracle to hinder.*
*Yet still the truth remains for everyone –*
*To King Jesus we shall all surrender.*

*Will you desire on this year's Christmas Day*
*To choose to put the Saviour Jesus first?*
*Decide to leave this empty worldly way*
*That heaven's glory on your soul may burst*
*And cause such worship that with Him you'll stay*
*And in His incarnation be immersed?*

My father loved to recite lots of poems from an ancient and now little known book called 'Merry Conceits.' He not only told them but acted them out, so that they became etched on our memories. I can still recite quite a few and with his same dramatic presentation. We had a billiard table to play on in the parish room which adjoined our house and there was table tennis in the church hall which we could use almost any time. There were high walls to climb on in and around our garden and we would jump from one to the other, completely unaware of any danger. Croquet would sometimes become polo as we rode round on our bikes, mallet in hand. The sea was just down the road where we could swim when we wanted to, except during the war. We could walk over the Downs or visit the villages or woods on our bikes, where very occasionally we were allowed to make camp.

We were thus in many ways very fortunate indeed, an experience remote from those who lived around us. However we were by no means rich and any money my father had to spare being spent on servants and private schooling. The décor of the house was pretty shabby and drab and in much need of repair or refurbishment. Nevertheless this was a home in which we could spread our wings and do exciting things. Whilst I was privileged in a way that was by no means common to all children, I was also left totally undomesticated and therefore ill prepared to be a housewife.

However, home life was also full of problems, largely stemming from my parents background. Still deeply hurt by the rejection of her father in India, a tragedy which instantaneously triggered severe insomnia, my mother was reliant on a strong drug called chloral. To this she added whiskey to increase its effectiveness, but sleep often eluded her. She would sometimes get up in the night, fall, bruise herself and end up with a black eye in the morning. On at least one occasion she attempted suicide with an overdose, but was thankfully saved by a stomach pump.

My father had a brilliant but highly strung and eccentric mother, who while at school, was awarded the prestigious prize for coming top of the whole country in both Latin and Greek. She was never cut out to be a mother and did not really understand children. My father was sent to Charterhouse and hated it as much if not more than my mother did her school, and often thought about running away. As an adult my father compensated for his emotional lack by throwing himself into parish life and gardening or butterflies as a hobby, in all of which he was totally absorbed. Thus, I believe, was avoided the hassle of establishing a deep relationship with my mother, which was of course, exactly what they both needed.

After only six weeks of marriage, my father could no longer stand my mother's insomnia and took himself off to another bedroom. Besides this, he kept my mother on a tight shoe string financially, so that she never knew how she would make ends meet with the meagre amount he gave her for housekeeping. This unnecessary anxiety and all these combined factors precipitated not only friction, but severe rows. Sometimes there would be tussles on the floor between my father and my teen aged brother. My brother, who has sadly recently died, had a furious temper and I lived in trepidation of him. On one occasion, as a prank, he was in the garden standing outside the open kitchen window with an air gun in his hands. I was inside next to a wall. Unbelievably he actually fired it at me, but as he cocked the gun, I quickly ducked! When I stood up, I saw a hole in the wall where my head would have been! I told my mother what had happened, but she did absolutely nothing about it, for I believe she too was frightened of him. My brother was a very complex character, highly intelligent and extremely gifted. Despite his volatile nature, he had a soft heart and an interest in needy people.

On more than one occasion I heard my mother

threaten to leave my father and quite often she would pack her bags as if to go. In my early and late teens, she would come into my bedroom in the middle of the night, crying and threatening to throw herself over Beachy Head. I had the painful task of trying to dissuade her, but I never mentioned this nightmare to anyone else. I was aware, and eventually told, that I was not a planned baby, coming so soon after the extremely premature arrival of my brother, who my mother had to fight to keep alive for many months. I therefore felt unwanted and grew up with many insecurities and fears, particularly that I would be poisoned. I became so nervous and tense that I was taken to a relaxation clinic in Brighton, until the war put an end to this therapy.

On one occasion my father took me out with him to catch butterflies in Abbots Wood, near where we lived in Eastbourne. He told me to sit down while he went off on his own, saying he would be back shortly. I was only a small child and it seemed that he was away for hours. I seriously thought that I had been abandoned like the Babes in the Wood. Another time, when I was only five years old father took me to see the great aunts who lived in Mulberry Walk in Chelsea. There were four of them and a great uncle called Sir Reginald Neville who was a member of parliament. On the train journey I went to the lavatory by myself, the train then stopped and when I came out my father had disappeared. He had got off the train at the correct station leaving me all alone in the vast metropolis of London. Precisely what happened next I cannot recall, except being utterly terrified.

My parents sent us all to boarding schools while very

young; I was just seven years old. Mother often used to collapse saying she was having a heart attack. She would always go the bed for one day each week and in the holidays we children were, in turn, given the privilege of looking after her. This involved bringing up her meals, creeping up to her bedroom so as not to wake her, and if awake, to rearrange her pillows, make her comfortable, stroke her face and kiss her. The holidays, however, always proved too long for her and she could not wait for them to end. "I can't cope!" was often on her lips, which left me with a sense of anxiety and rejection.

At meals my father would suddenly put his hand sharply under our elbows and bellow; "all joints on the table should be carved!" This might have seemed amusing to him, but I found it an unexpected and unwelcome shock to the system. Once my mother, for no apparent reason, took a carpet beater and gave me a hiding. I very nearly made a rope out of my sheets to lower myself from my bedroom window into the garden and run for it, but I thought better of the idea. My mother was a good listener and in some ways very psychologically progressive but she only ever seemed to want to hear about my woes and not about my successes. My father was a distant and rather to be feared figure. I can never ever remember sitting on his lap or being cuddled by him. At the age of thirteen I became unusually bold one day; I was walking down the stairs, with him standing at the bottom. I announced slowly and with great depth of emotion; "I do not know you." This really said it all, but there was no response.

Many years later, after I had been happily married for

quite a long time and had well-adjusted children, my mother remarked with obvious pleasure how surprised she was at the way I managed. She was interested to find out the reason. I tried to explain to her that the credit for this was not due to me, for by myself I would have been incapable, but it lay in the goodness and mercy of the Lord and His gracious help. Thankfully neither of my parents ever interfered in my marriage or child rearing. My father in his retirement and with time now to spare began to open up to me, particularly over spiritual matters. We had many wonderful discussions which drew us much closer together. He gained a respect for me which became increasingly evident.

Looking back now and with hindsight, I wish I had spent more time enquiring about my parent's childhood; their pain and how they felt about it in their latter years. I could have shown so much more empathy. I could have used the skills I had by then acquired in counselling. I could have been so much more of a comfort to them. No one can put the clock back, but thankfully the Saviour can cleanse and forgive our sins of omission, teach us through our failures and create in us softer hearts for hurting people, especially those close to us.

# War breaks out

# CHAPTER 3

"You shall hear of wars and rumours of wars. See that you are not troubled." Matthew 24.6

Grim faced my parents told me that war had been declared. They had just heard Mr. Chamberlain's speech on the radio. I wondered what all the fuss was about when they told us the news. I remember exclaiming, "How exciting!" to which they replied, "You know nothing ... you have no idea." I was only a little girl of six, quite ignorant of the horrors of war, whereas they had both gone through the First World War during their early teens and knew only too well.

Then began the preparation for war in our town and it eventually became clear that Eastbourne was not a safe place in which to live. The reason was that we were on the line of Operation Sealion, the very area of England that the Germans planned to invade. Barbed wire was erected along the sea front; mines planted so that no one could use the beaches, iron railings surrounding buildings were requisitioned by the government and sent to factories to be used for ammunitions and armaments. Sign posts were also removed, street lights became a thing of the past and the few cars permitted on the roads were not allowed to use their lights at night, making travelling extremely hazardous.

Each family also made their own preparations. At night all windows had to be blackened, so that not even a peep of light should shine through, and were also covered with strips of sticky paper to lessen the impact of shattered glass. Morrison air raid shelters were given to those most in need, which did not include us – we had a strong cellar with a room beneath a flight of sturdy stone steps in which to retire to relative safety. This room happened to be our laundry room and so had running water and electricity and there was just enough room for each of us to sit in a chair and to store essentials such as food, first aid items and blankets.

Ration books were then handed out, for both food and clothes. The black market thrived and my mother exchanged money for food and clothing coupons with our own char lady who spent it on 'fags'. Porridge was placed in a hay box overnight to cook itself and everything that could be preserved was put into special water glass bottles, including eggs, for we not only had a large vegetable garden and an orchard, but also kept chickens. Mother decided to buy a goat to provide extra milk, but I do not think this brain wave lasted long! Living by the sea meant there was a small supply of fish for which there was no rationing. When the signal was given, everyone rushed to the fishmonger where you could be sure of a long queue. Generally food was sufficient if care was taken and it proved to be a very balanced and healthy diet. There were no obesity problems like there are today and no one starved. As the merchant ships were unable to bring foods such as oranges and bananas, sandwiches were made with cooked mashed parsnips with a little banana essence added. Ham sandwiches consisted of bread and margarine, a sprinkle of salt and pepper and a dab of mustard! Clothes were made out of whatever was available; mother made us all dressing gowns out of blankets.

Soon the reality of war really began to hit us, as German planes came over from France, (usually but not always), on their way to London. If they had any bombs left over on their return journey they would drop them on Eastbourne. There were also the 'tip and run' raids with little or no warning. My father became an air raid warden and I remember the scared look on his face as he ventured out of our front door to do his work. A special type of air raid siren was used in Eastbourne called the Cuckoo. By the time the cuckoo had sounded three times, we could be sure that the German bombers would be overhead. Up we would get as quickly as possible and rush down to the basement cellar, collecting our gas masks on the way. I was always first as I was a light sleeper and also because I was exceedingly frightened. After each raid we would go and look through the upstairs windows to see fires burning around us. Several incendiary bombs landed on our church primary school at the bottom of our garden, almost completely obliterating it. Another bomb landed in the recreation ground in front of our house, but nothing ever touched us.

One day mother went to buy a pair of shoes for me; she was allowed to take one shoe for me to try on at home. As she arrived home, a raid began. When the all clear sounded, she went back to collect the other shoe and to her amazement, the shoe shop no longer existed. It had received a direct hit. What a narrow escape my mother surely had! As the war grew increasingly dangerous, all we children went to boarding schools in the relative safety of the countryside, but the holidays back in Eastbourne still presented a problem. I was evacuated to a vicarage in Dorset where the son of a vicar started making advances to me. Being only eleven years old and totally innocent of his intentions towards me, I agreed to go up with him to the top of the church tower. There he sexually assaulted me, though by the mercy of God, never raped me. I managed to escape his clutches and ran helter-skelter down the rickety steps trembling with fear. I had nowhere to go but back to the vicarage with him following hard on my heels. Within days psoriasis covered my body. Our cousin, the Reverend Shackleton, a relative of Sir Ernest Shackleton, lived with his spinster sister in a little village in Shropshire called Bedstone, and fortunately he agreed to have us all to stay in his vicarage. My father remained at home, while the rest of us, including our living in maid, evacuated westwards.

We stayed there for a while, but eventually my mother could not stand Miss Shackleton's unfortunate habit of kleptomania a moment longer and decided to leave. She spoke to the squire, Sir Henry Ripley, who kindly let us use half of one of his Elizabethan cottages. The other half was occupied by a farm labourer and his wife and I remember there always being a pig hung and cured in their inglenook. Our half of the cottage had no running water and only one cold tap in an open passageway leading to a small garden. Therefore all water had to be collected from this one tap and if needed, boiled up in a large kettle on the inglenook fire for both cooking and bathing. An old zinc bath was placed in front of the fire and filled, and needless to say, we all took turns to use the same water.

Bedstone was situated in the heart of the most beautiful countryside. My brother and I, for my sister was only a baby, used to bicycle to all sorts of exciting places; we would swim in rivers, climb trees, pick wild raspberries from the woods, collect sloe berries and gather mushrooms from the fields. One time my mother and our maid were with us when we walked across a field with my sister in a pram surrounded by lumps of coal we had picked up from the railway line. Suddenly a bull rushed towards us and how we managed to clamber over the fence in time with the heavily weighted pram, I do not know, but it was surely the Lord's protection.

Everyone eligible had to enlist in the armed forces, or if they were conscientious objectors, they were relegated to the coal mines; that is except; 'the blind, the mentally deficient and ministers of religion'! Thus my father escaped mandatory enlistment. He was allowed a motor bike to look after his flock left in Eastbourne and also those members who had been scattered by evacuation, largely into the West Country. Occasionally he would drive on to Shropshire and see the family.

Later on in the war, because the Battle of Britain had been won and it was considerably less dangerous, we all went back to Eastbourne for the holidays. Bombs were still being dropped on the town though, and I still vividly remember when I was once out in the garden and a

German plane swooped over. The pilot tried to take a pot-shot at me as I rushed indoors, my legs never carrying me faster while I shook like a jelly fish, for I had even seen his face!

To this very day, my nerves remain somewhat frayed when a plane flies low or creates an unexpectedly loud noise. The effects of war do not completely go away, for like all other traumas, they are etched into our genes and registered there. The Lord can take away fear, which He indeed does, and has done for me. "I sought the Lord and He heard me and delivered me from all my fears." Ps 34.4. However, the emotional and physical reaction towards past experiences may not change. I learned a great deal by going through the Second World War; I learned about camaraderie, unselfishness, self-control, sacrifice and how to make a little go a long way so that ends would meet. Our minds had been expanded to think creatively, which was indeed essential for survival. This experience taught me many lessons that have proved invaluable in my life. Above all, I discovered the Lord's goodness in protecting and preserving all my family intact, for which I give Him thanks and praise.

# An adventurous spirit is born

CHAPTER

4

"The people that know their God shall be bold and do great exploits." Daniel 11.32

Slowly moving towards the Bishop's Eye, the stone vaulted exit from the palace grounds, she walked, turning round every now and then to wave another goodbye. Then she was gone and I was alone standing there outside the drawbridge. Strangely, I did not shed a tear, for it was I who had told my mother, "You can go home now, I will be all right." I imagine this reaction must have greatly relieved her as she had been keen to get me out of war torn Eastbourne and into the comparative safety of Wells Palace, to which my school, St. Brandon's had been evacuated from the bombing of Bristol.

I returned across the drawbridge under which there was a moat which went right round the palace gardens. Swans there would ring a bell for food by using their beaks to pull a cord. I went back through the gate house, across an immaculate lawn to the imposing pink-grey stone palace, through some stone passages and into a large dining hall supported by huge stone pillars where lunch was being served. I had only just turned seven, but somehow I felt a thrill of excitement tingling through me. My adventure had begun and I relished the thought of it.

I was given a pale blue aertex blouse and navy shorts which made me feel very grown up, because all the other girls, who were much older than I, had this uniform on too. I was, in fact the only young child there at the time. The head mistress, Miss Nora Almond, whose forebears had founded the Glenalmond and Loretto public schools, was a distant relative of ours, and although I had never met her, mother thought I would be safe in her hands. The first night came and the long gallery, (known to us as the whispering gallery), had been turned into a large dormitory full of children. There were large paintings hanging on the walls of eminent people of bygone years and it was rumoured that a lady in white stepped out of one of the pictures and was seen wandering around as a ghost.

Not long after this, I was moved to the preparatory school at Milton Lodge, up in the Mendip hills. This was a beautiful house in an enchanting setting, having a stunning view in the valley below of most of the cathedral and the entire spire. There was an enormous, varied and interesting garden which was ideal for children to play in and pursue all sorts of interesting activities. I had moved from the palace, but I had not bidden farewell to my new adventure for as yet I was only on its threshold. Although Milton Lodge was a big imposing house, everything appeared to be on a much smaller scale than at the palace, as was the case. This created a more friendly and homely environment. The Headmistress, Miss Dobbie, loved and understood children. She encouraged an indomitable courageous spirit of adventure as well as fun. Thus I, being a rebel at heart, was not meted out the punishments deserved for frequently breaking school rules.

We were allowed to pack and unpack our trunks unsupervised and so I was able to smuggle in a home-made rope ladder my father had made me. No one even knew of its existence except my three friends, Celia Swann, Ann Morris and Susan Hall. Together we went out of bounds to a wood where there was a gigantic old beech tree. We slung the rope ladder over the lowest branch, clambered up it, eased our way to the trunk and finally made it right to the top. We were all experienced tree climbers. I believe this tree was almost as tall as the cathedral with its spire. We were never found out and so we continued this hazardous escapade several times.

On another occasion we managed to sneak some food out of the kitchen, somehow finding matches to light a fire and under a hedge we tried to cook a meal. Then followed Miss Colinett's catechism lesson where we learned about the necessity of repentance. We all felt very convicted and so we went to her after the lesson to confess our crime. Being wise, she considered the act of confession sufficient and did not hand out any punishment. One day, Celia, Susan. Ann and I conceived a very dangerous enterprise; carefully planned against any detection and executed with some trepidation. At dead of night we crept out of our beds and climbed out of a window onto the narrow ledge that surrounded the house and walked right round it. On this occasion we were caught and punished and it was surprising that we were not expelled.

A path led down from the house to the stables and halfway along it was a very steep bank. At its top were willow trees with their myriads of long dangling branches.

These proved to be excellent fun as we could cling onto them and swing from the top to the bottom and then jump off. There was some element of danger, but nevertheless, this exhilaration we were allowed to enjoy. Night times were exciting too; there were stories told ever so quietly after lights-out and we competed to tell the most gruesome ones. We would play the game; 'truth, dare or force' and egg each other on do the most outrageous things, such as running naked into the kitchens to steal food. If we heard footsteps outside the dormitory, the expression *cave* was used, (meaning be careful in Latin and pronounced KV.) Sometimes a teacher would come in and announce, "Gillian Marcon and Patsy Lane, you may come and have staff supper." These were left overs, but eagerly relished by us children. We would leap out of bed with alacrity, but only those with strong stomachs were ever given this privilege and fortunately I was one of them. You see, everything had to be eaten up. There could be no wastage and we were not allowed to leave the table until the plate was empty, for merchant seamen were risking their lives to bring us food in the war. This meant, for instance, having to swallow revolting tapioca which looked like frogspawn and made us vomit. I would put mine in my handkerchief and then into my pocket ever hopeful that no one would see!

After staff supper on sunny warm evenings we would be asked to pick carrots, beans, lettuces and all sorts of other vegetables from the kitchen garden. We loved doing this as it was hard to sleep in the summer heat. In the winter, the headmistress would invite the older children to her sitting room where a blazing log fire burned in the grate. She would read adventure stories like Enid Blyton's Famous Five or other well-known classics, like The Children of the New Forest and Scott of the Antarctic. What fun we also had building pine needle villages under the old cedar tree and making houses in the field out of bamboos interwoven with hay. There were wonderful walks in the Mendip hills, sometimes trails being laid for 'Hares and Hounds.' On these walks I became captivated by the appeal of nature, learning to differentiate between the species of wild flowers, trees, butterflies, birds and their eggs and so on. We also visited Wookey Hole and Cheddar Gorge, seeing the stalagmites and the stalactites.

When I was ten, (but in a class of mostly eleven year olds, because Miss Dobbie did not want to separate me from my friends), we moved back to the senior school in Wells. On returning I was once again immersed in the ambience of the ancient buildings of the palace and the cathedral where we would sometimes worship on Sundays. The music enthralled me and I was enraptured in this setting. I even imagined myself to be a young Bach, particularly because I had started to compose music on the piano, which I usually did at weekends and sometimes for hours on end. The greatest risk we four girls ever took could again have cost us our lives; we climbed up the palace tower one night and onto the high narrow wall surrounding the gardens, with a forty foot drop to the moat below. We were caught, again sent to the headmistress, severely reprimanded and very nearly expelled. I believe that one of St Brandon's principal aims was to make school as exciting as possible and also to encourage and instil self-reliance, confidence and prowess. Thus was born this longing for adventure, perhaps inherited from my cousin Sir Ernest Shackleton, (the Antarctic explorer) but certainly developed by my experiences in this distinctly avant-garde setting. A latent spirit of adventure was awakened deep within my bones. Sadly however, I was plucked from this exciting environment and sent to three different schools after reaching the age of fourteen, none of which fostered this same spirit.

A day would come when I would no longer desire or choose to risk my life doing foolish forbidden pranks. Instead, as I got to know my Lord and Saviour better, I would be encouraged to be bold and to do exploits ... for Him, who shed his blood and gave His life for me.

## Adventurous Spirit

*Adventure; this is what I seek,*
*Not life the same each day.*
*Not dull or boring, never weak*
*For dragons I will slay.*

*Adventure's mine if I will take*
*Fresh courage in my hand.*
*The best life surely I will make,*
*A life that's never bland.*

*I'll go to places no one dares,*
*Endure the hardest things.*
*For what is life if full of cares*
*That miss exciting things?*

*Adventurous spirit, that is mine,*
*Which none from me can flush.*
*No one my spirit can confine,*
*Nor e'er succeed to crush.*

*For deep within's a flint-like soul*
*That will not ever move*
*Or conquered be, for I've a goal,*
*And something worth to prove.*

# The magic of music

"Praise the Lord with the sound of the trumpet. Praise Him on the tambourine and harp. Praise Him with stringed instruments and the organ. Praise Him with loud cymbals." Psalm 150: 3–5

How the magic of music drew me irresistibly, like a magnet! I qualify the word magic as here meaning only the wonderfully exciting and exhilarating effect music has upon the soul. Had I been able, I would have listened to the music that rang through the cathedral and palace for hours. I was enraptured and transported into another realm, a world of which hitherto I knew practically nothing. This was because my mother considered music to be an unnecessary noise and Bach nothing more than five finger exercises. Hence music was rarely if ever heard in our home until my brother and I learned to play the piano.

At the palace I was allowed to have piano lessons straight away and was privileged to be able to use the chapel's grand piano. Then having moved to Milton Lodge, I learned with a most inspirational teacher called Margaret Pye. By the time I was nine years old I had reached grade five and I remember playing "The song of the lark," by Tchaikovsky. I was then sent to a concert pianist, but alas in my dreaminess, I forgot to turn up to my lessons regularly and had to forfeit this opportunity. I was put back with my original teacher at the preparatory school, which was no bad thing, for I do not believe I could have had anyone better. One discipline she set her pupils each week and which proved to be of great value later on, was in the form of a competition. Each child was given a manuscript showing single notes ranging from the top to the bottom of the keyboard, which we had to try to play as quickly as possible. This enabled me to become a very fast sight reader!

While I was still only about nine years old, in music class at school we were taught all about the early classical and then the romantic composers. The life stories of Mozart, Bach and Beethoven (perhaps the most famous of all the composers) were read to us and these geniuses from the past literally became alive. We were taught how to distinguish between each, so that even if we had not heard a particular work before, we could recognise its style and identify its composer. For instance, Mozart and Haydn's music are very similar, but Haydn's tends to be more up-beat and consistently happy, whereas Mozart's has more pathos and can evoke feelings of sadness. We were taught how to distinguish between the different instruments of the orchestra, for instance that an oboe sounds something like a clarinet, with a cold in its nose!

I was privileged to learn the violin with Fraulein Bower, a pupil of Kreisler, the famous violinist of the day. She had been the leader of the Vienna Philharmonic Orchestra, but being Jewish, had fled the Nazis and fortunately for us, had come to St Brandon's. The lessons with her proved to be excruciating agony as she pulled my left shoulder back, stretched my fingers on the strings and then pressed them in until grooves appeared on the tips! No one was allowed to learn with her unless they had perfect pitch, so I was honoured indeed. Sadly and to my chagrin, I have to confess that I did not practice according to her strict demands and again, as with the concert pianist, I forfeited this priceless opportunity. Concerts were held each term at the school and the girls were able to contribute their musical talents. I remember at the age of twelve playing the first movement of Beethoven's Pathetique Sonata, a piece that demonstrates great contrast and drama. When I had finished playing, everyone stood up and clapped. Being most definitely a 'show off,' I loved this accolade! We also had excellent class singing lessons in which we were taught to sing in harmony and to produce as clear and pure a voice as possible.

When I left school at seventeen I needed two 'A' levels for university. I was then living at home and I chose music as one of them. I decided to do this in the November and so only had seven months to complete the course. I obtained the syllabus, found that I had already completed the practical piano grade needed and was left with four other parts to study. One of these was harmony, which I learned with our church organist and found easy because I had the advantage of already composing. The oral was a doddle because I had perfect pitch and that left me with history of music and the set works. For the former I almost swallowed the entire Oxford Companion to Music by Scholes and for the latter, all I had were the scores. No one even thought to buy me a record and in fact I did not hear them played until much later on when I was married. My friend Joan, who later taught music as a career and who had been able to hear the works played, took the exam with me at the high school. She surprisingly failed whilst I got a distinction! Perhaps the papers got muddled up?

When I had children of my own, I organised piano and singing lessons for them. Each one then branched out with their preferred instruments. My son, Andrew and my second daughter Sarah both learned five instruments including singing, and my elder daughter Rachel learned three. Both Sarah and Andrew passed their seventh or eighth grade in each instrument. I insisted that they practice each day and practice properly. Our large vicarage afforded enough space for two pianos, which was very helpful. Our children regularly entered the Tunbridge Wells Music Festival in a wide variety of disciplines, ranging from drama to music and would often achieve first place. Andrew won the prized Entertainer's Cup when he was ten years old, having entered the piano, violin, singing, drama, poetry and bible reading classes and coming top in each. A celebration lunch was held at the Swan Hotel in his honour, with the Mayor being present.

My husband, Tony has always encouraged the children with their music and loves to listen to classical music, but does not play any instrument himself. By the time the children had reached the ages of three, six and eight, they could sing merrily in three part unaccompanied harmony. Various songs would be performed at home and especially on long car journeys. The children just loved music and it was ever present in our home, even at night when they went off to bed I purposely left their bedroom doors open so that they could hear strains wafting up from downstairs, before falling asleep.

In 1977, the Queen's Silver Jubilee year, I was watching the television one day and I heard that the Chorister of Great Britain competition was to be held in November. It was to be run by The Royal School of Church Music together with Rediffusion Television. The prize would be one thousand pounds for the winner's church and to enter you had to be a boy in a church choir. As our church choir consisted of young teenage girls, men and women and no boys, this posed a problem. A talented singer like Andrew surely could not miss an opportunity like this and so I asked the choir master if he would admit him into the choir. There was some reluctance, but eventually he agreed. For the majority of the next few months I taught Andrew myself but soon realised that he would need more expert help. We found Mr. John, a professor from the Guild Hall School of Music, who was an excellent teacher.

The first hurdle was passed when Andrew was selected to sing in Bath Abbey. Out of 3,000 boys who were auditioned at different venues nationwide, just twelve were chosen. Andrew was one of them! The set piece for the competition was Mendelssohn's 'O for the wings of a dove' and Andrew chose Bach's 'Bist du bei mir' for his second. Ernest Lough, the famous boy soprano who was known to millions for his recording of 'O for the wings'... in 'Hear my prayer' in the 1920's was actually one of the adjudicators. The other was Sir David Wilcox, the principal of the Royal College of Music. After the contest and before the results were announced, we were wined and dined at the Mayfair Hotel. Vodka was surreptitiously added to my bitter lemon with the remark, "You will need this!" Not being at all accustomed to alcohol, I could barely walk a straight line to collect food from the buffet! Then at last it was time for the judges' decision which was read out in reverse order. After the first two were announced I whispered to Andrew, "You've won," and joy of joys, he had!

The next day, having spent the night at the hotel we were taken off by car at break-neck speed to various studios so that Andrew could perform and record footage for the media. Because of union rules, his pianist was not permitted to play for him. I had to step into the breach at a moment's notice and accompany him for one of the programmes which was to be shown on television. There was such a hullaballoo going on behind me on the stage, people talking and camera's clicking, that in exasperation I stood up, turned round and announced; "When you have all finished, I will proceed!" Silenced reigned!

The following day, the seven o'clock news opened with Andrew singing. Frustratingly, we experienced a power cut which meant that we missed most of it! Nevertheless there was a celebration luncheon again with the mayor, to enjoy at the Alpine Rose Hotel in Tunbridge Wells. We were sent newspaper cuttings and letters from all over the world, some only addressed to 'Andrew March, Tunbridge Wells,' or 'Andrew March, chorister of Great Britain.' Andrew was offered a place at the Royal College of Music by Sir David Wilcox for the following year, by which time Andrew's voice would have matured. He told the media

"Andrew's voice is one of the most flawless voices I have ever heard and has a maturity beyond it's years." Sadly he never took up music as a career and eventually became an osteopath. However, for a while he was the director of music at Kensington Temple; a large church in London with several thousand members. Rachel and Sarah are both involved with leading music at their local churches.

The magic of music has thus gripped our family and although none of us have taken it up professionally, it has remained a beautiful relaxation, a solace and an inspiration to the soul. However, the music of earth can never match or surpass the music of heaven, which is beyond our wildest dreams. The nearest we can get to this down here is when we 'sing psalms and hymns and spiritual songs,' (Eph 5.19) with others or on our own; the love songs which the Lord has put in our hearts for Him.

## Music

*Music ringing through cathedral*
*And the palace chapel too.*
*Drew me as compelling magnet,*
*Touched my heart strings through and through.*

*Pealing organ thundering grandly,*
*Reaching every corner, 'till*
*Only music then be heard here*
*With it's never ending thrill.*

As I listened, held me spellbound,
To new realms transported me.
Left me speechless at its beauty
Never quite the same to be.

Soaring upwards went my spirit,
Inspiration to my soul,
Solace found in such a mystery
Is beyond me to extol.

But the music of men's making
Can't compare in any way
With the glory of the music
Under God's almighty sway.

For in heaven's the finest music,
Where the angels love to sing.
Every instrument is found there,
All to God their worship bring.

Music God has put within us,
Placed deep down some special songs.
Tell them out; tell out His glory
For to Him our praise belongs.

# A medical student – with no scientific foundation

"We know that all things work together for good to those ... who are called according to His purpose." Romans 8.28

"Gill Marcon, lift up your mattress." matron yelled. Reluctantly I obeyed. "And *what* are all those things doing hidden under there?" I fumbled awkwardly to find words and then decided to be bold, because after all I had already been found out. "These are here to help anyone who is sick or needs help in my dormitory" I answered sheepishly. There carefully concealed, or so I thought, was my special first aid box of plasters, bandages and creams and other lotions and potions. "What *do* you think you are doing? You know perfectly well this is not allowed!" My precious medical kit was confiscated and I was left devastated. At the age of only nine the beginnings of my dreams to be a doctor were dashed.

I also had some problems at school. The teachers would often tell me to stop looking out of the window and concentrate. I believe my lack of concentration was the result of a subconscious anxiety stemming from my early childhood. Alas I never wanted to read and never did until it was forced upon me by impending 'O' level exams. My passion for music, sport, nature and above all adventure absorbed me and thus I came bottom in most subjects, though strangely always top in scripture.

When I left school at seventeen, mother suggested I trained as a nanny and insisted I try St. Christopher's in Tunbridge Wells, to which we paid a visit. The very idea of being a nanny made me shudder! "No, I want to be a doctor," I firmly told her. You see, my parents thought my older brother was the clever one not me, and he had tried medicine and failed, so what chance had I? They also thought I was simply being a copy-cat! Dick was in actual fact cleverer than I, but I think he suffered from a condition called dyspraxia; an inability to write fast enough and so he could not complete the exam papers. I continued to make frantic pleas and was eventually sent to the Child Guidance clinic in Eastbourne for an IQ test. The result was unexpected as I had failed two important 'O' Level exams and did only moderately well in the re-sits. When my parents told me that my IQ was one mark under Mensa, they were not only surprised, but they did not have a leg to stand on, especially as the clinic openly encouraged my ambition. The first hurdle was to matriculate and get a Statement of Eligibility for university. I now had to get the right grades in English and French. My parents kindly let me stay at home for a year and found me excellent teachers for both subjects. I remember learning my brother's essays by heart, hoping I might get a question on one of them. He excelled at English, whereas this was my 'bête noire.' I also needed two 'A' levels, so I decided to take one in music, along with the French and English 'O' levels.

I had had a serious motor bike accident when I went out riding with my father at the age of eleven which took its toll on my health. Back at school, following this event and presumably to aid recuperation I was made to go to bed every maths and latin lesson, and hence I was left mathematically illiterate. I have no idea what thinking lay behind this bizarre decision, for it seems quite extraordinarily stupid to allow a child to miss out on such an important subject as maths! Mother, however found me an Oxbridge coach and in the only six weeks available before starting university, I reached 'O' level standard in both arithmetic and algebra. She told me that I was her best pupil ever! The only reason I managed to learn so fast was my dogged determination to become a doctor. I believe no one really utilizes their full intelligence potential until desire or need extracts more of what is latent.

When the time came to apply to medical school, I went round by bus and by foot to every London teaching hospital personally begging entry and received three interviews. The day King George VI died was a red letter day for me, because on it I received an acceptance. I am quite sure I was only given a place because the Dean of the medical school, noted my unusual surname, Marcon. He asked me whether I was related to his friend Sholto Marcon with whom he had played all England hockey, which I told him was indeed the case.

I now needed a second 'A' level and so the next year I went to a crammer in London called Borland's, where I chose to study Zoology and Botany taken as one exam, Biology. Happily I entered both the London and Oxford exam boards, for I failed the London exam and got a distinction in the Oxford! There are two particular memories worth mentioning here and one is that at Borland's we had a sweepstake. Now my father was very opposed to any form of gambling, even 'a little flutter,' as he would call it, but I went weakly along with everyone else and put money on the bet, though feeling rather guilty and wishing that I had not done so. When the winner was announced and it was me, I was mortified and handed the money straight back, to the bewilderment of the organizers! These were "ill-gotten gains," I heard my father's words ringing in my ears.

The second memory of that place was sitting opposite a very thin, emaciated, cadaverous young man while doing practical Zoology. I found him repulsive and usually managed to avoid him. When I heard later on that he had been in the infamous Belsen concentration camp, I hated myself for this reaction. I wish I could have gone back in time and shown the compassion he deserved which I withheld because of my inability to do so at that time in my life.

How I managed to get a place at medical school without maths 'O' level was incredible enough, but this was not the only gap in my education. I had virtually no knowledge of chemistry or physics, both of which were required subjects. It took me just over two years to scrape through First MB. Because of the system in place then, I ended up taking the equivalent of A level Biology five times and I think I could have dissected a dogfish blindfold! The next hurdle was Second MB; here the problem was that I had only absorbed 'physical' chemistry. Biochemistry which is an integral part of Second MB, is based on 'organic' chemistry which in turn is built on 'inorganic' chemistry, neither of which had I scarcely any acquaintance. I did not really know the periodic table! My first lecture in physiology was taken up with the dangers of smoking, which was very avant-garde at the time. That very day I stopped smoking and have never smoked again.

I was not only up against a lack of basic scientific knowledge, but I also had to contend with London's worst recorded smog which killed ten thousand people in 1952. Unaware that it might be dangerous, I walked through London in this 'pea-souper,' contracted a serious form of pneumonia and nearly died, which put me behind with my studies. Furthermore the lump sum my father had given me to pay for my training was not going to be sufficient to cover any more exam re-takes, which I concluded were inevitable. Thus I realised that I had met my 'waterloo' and with very great sadness I abandoned my dream. I had enjoyed every minute of being a medical student, I had learned a great deal and above all, I was being led to life's greatest choice, upon which my eternal destiny depended.

## Meeting the King of Kings

"He has on His robe and on His thigh a name written;
King of Kings and Lord of Lords." Revelation 19.16

I came from a long line of clergymen, about twenty six altogether. My father was an Anglo-Catholic and went to Cuddesdon Theological College in Oxford. He was a godly man, but believed that the Bible only contained the word of God, and was not all the actual word of God.

St. Brandon's school was a Church of England clergy daughter's school where I was taught scripture by Miss Read who made the Bible come alive and learned to sing scriptural verses, despite the liberal stance of the school. I learned the Acts of the Apostles almost by heart and always came top in scripture exams, but bottom in all other subjects except music, at which I excelled. It was here that I began to ponder God's love.

### Behold His love

*Behold the Lamb of God who came*
*To this dark sinful world of shame;*
*Behold His love for you and me,*
*The sinless Son to set us free.*

*Behold the nail pierced feet and hands,*
*The riven side, the cruel bands.*

*Behold the silent Lamb at trial,*
*Condemned by trumped up lies so vile;*
*Behold His love and wondrous grace*
*To take my penalty and place;*
*Behold the heart that was so torn,*
*Cut off from Father God, forlorn.*

*Behold the Lamb to suffering goes,*
*To battering by a thousand blows;*
*Behold such love – took punishment,*
*When I to hell should have been sent.*
*Behold the ugly crown of thorns,*
*The mocking, insults and the scorns.*

*Behold the Lamb for murderers prays,*
*In quiet obedience now He stays;*
*Behold His love – to shed His blood,*
*And in my place convicted stood;*
*Behold the pain and agony*
*Of Jesus dying there for me.*

*Behold His love; behold it till*
*Upon my knees, my tears I spill;*
*Behold His love - until I break,*
*And at the cross His will I take.*
*Behold His love; behold his love;*
*My Saviour and my God above.*

At the age of nine I wrote in the middle of an exercise book just three words in bold red letters, GOD IS LOVE. Nothing else was ever written in this book. I had begun a yearning for this God of love, but no one told me how I could find Him. I used to pray by my bed at boarding school and slippers were thrown at me by the girls who told that I would end up as a nun! As was normal in the Church of England, I was baptised as a baby and confirmed as a teenager. I went to church regularly and I imagined I was a pretty good girl!

There was, however a dark secret in my life which lived to haunt me for the next twelve years. All the girls had clubbed together to teach one particular girl a lesson and they chose me to execute it. This poor child was all by herself and feeling very frightened and alone up at the main house, Milton Lodge, whilst the rest of us were down at the stables. I was told to go and get her and pretend that all would be fine if she came along with me, when in reality something quite horrible was planned. Without a thought, I fell in with this foul scheme; on the way to the stables the girl and I passed by a steep embankment covered with stinging nettles. As it was summer time we were only wearing shorts. Suddenly and unexpectedly for her, I gave her a huge push and she fell down the embankment and was stung all over. I only wish I knew who this poor victim was so that I could say sorry, but I have never discovered. This obnoxious behaviour, something I did not dream could be in my nature, because I had never done such a thing before or have done since, led me to think about good and evil. I was guilty of deceit, connivance and violence, but was there any goodness in me? I thus devised a method to discover where I stood, and in a small book I had pages to tick when I was good and to cross when I was bad.

It was not until I went up to London University to study medicine, lodging in a Salvation Army hostel and joining the Medical School Christian Union, that I began to realise that something was radically wrong inside me. Something was strangely missing that others seemed to possess. I was meeting people who knew the Lord Jesus Christ personally. They kindly took me to good Bible believing churches where the gospel was preached and the Word of God was explained. I was taken to Westminster Chapel on Sunday mornings and to All Souls, Langham Place on Sunday evenings.

## The Preacher

*He stands there quietly at preaching desk,*
*Tall figure, shoulders broad, and smilingly,*
*With knee pressed in as each word coming next*
*Is uttered with precision, carefully.*
*No noise disturbs the place, and with his text*
*He pleads with everyone so lovingly.*

*He stands there, what a giant of a man!*
*With frequent tears acquainted; passionately,*
*With burning fear of God before him, can*
*False arguments demolish cogently –*
*Conceived in opposition to God's plan.*
*Thus speaks the preacher to us urgently.*

*He stands there resolute, with thoughts abreast*
*Of all that makes men stagger; foolishly*
*Reject the Lord, and thus with Him contest.*
*With reasonings clear and deep, he fearlessly*
*Proclaims that sin God really does detest,*
*And urges all, this ponder seriously.*

*He stands to then explain God's saving grace*
*With clarity and power, appealingly –*
*Shows Jesus paid the price for human race*
*Upon the cross, His blood shed willingly.*
*God's wrath appeased, when Jesus took our place,*
*So sin could be expunged amazingly.*

*He stands, another Paul before us set,*
*With book in hand, he beckons longingly,*
*Sees if the message has convinced us yet:*
*Asks whether we've received believingly?*
*The Saviour of the world have truly met?*
*He waits and prays, that God works inwardly.*

*He stands and we are privileged to hear*
*This man of God, who's suffered shamefully,*
*Denying all that this world holds most dear;*
*To take the cross and follow willingly*
*His Lord; which ever way He leads, makes clear.*
*Lord, may we too, serve You as faithfully.*

I heard the great Biblical truths of Substitutionary Atonemant, Justification by grace alone through faith, the New Birth, the New Heart and the New Life, these being inseparably linked with holiness. Yet all these truths seemed to go over my head, or rather my heart, and nothing had changed in my life. Nevertheless, a very firm foundation was being laid.

I began to be very fearful of being in a train accident when travelling back and forth between Eastbourne and London. I knew if I were to die, I would have to face the Judge of the whole earth, and I was not ready. I had this phrase of Dr. Martin Lloyd Jones repeating in my mind and which he prayed without fail each Sunday morning; *'this short uncertain life.'* The Lord was now deeply troubling my conscience. I began searching the Bible with more diligence. I attended Bible studies and prayer meetings at the Salvation Army hostel and the Christian Union at the medical school. I avidly read Inter Varsity Fellowship publications and missionary biographies. Every spare minute was precious.

I now faced the daunting task of getting through my medical studies and simultaneously trying to find the Lord. Each vied with me for attention and absorbed my mind. This forced me to cut out many activities, both social and physical, to afford enough time to devote to the intense search which had begun. I was also in a dilemma, for what I had been taught as a child was contrary in several respects to what I was now learning. The question loomed; which was right? My mother gave me a book called "The Cloud of Unknowing," which did not prove to be very helpful, for I was now under teaching that we *could* know, we *should* know and we *must* know. It took me three years to unravel all this, but I was unwittingly following a scriptural exhortation to "Search with all your heart and then you will find Me." Jer 29.13

It was Good Friday, just after my twenty-first birthday, and I was at home in bed reading the Bible when I stumbled on Genesis 6; 3 and it arrested me. "My Spirit will not strive with man for ever." Into my mind popped an old hymn, 'Once to every man and nation comes the moment to decide.' I leapt out of bed and onto my knees and for the first time I realised that although I believed in God and that Jesus was the only Saviour, He was standing there *outside* my life. I found myself looking at the picture by Holman Hunt, a present from my brother, which was hanging on the wall. There was Jesus standing outside a door with a lantern. I saw that He had both a crown of thorns and a crown of glory. I saw that the door was covered with weeds and that it had no handle on the outside and I saw Jesus knocking patiently. At that moment I knew that Jesus was right there with me.

There, on my knees I was before Jesus. He was shedding His light into my heart, exposing the awfulness of my sin, revealing that He was not only the Saviour but also the Lord, who had a right to the throne of my life. Very gently He was asking me to let Him come in and forgive me, and that I had to make the choice. I burst into tears and wept uncontrollably for a very long time. I told Him how sorry I was for the life I had led without Him. I told Him I never wanted to live the same way again. I truly repented and offered my life unreservedly to Him. I said, "Lord Jesus, please take away my sin and wash me clean. Please come in and take over my life. I need You so desperately." And, you know He did just that! He came into my life that very moment, exactly as He had promised, for he said, not I *might*, but "…I *will* come in." Rev 3.20

I arose a completely new person; totally new. I was washed clean in His blood and I was filled with His Spirit. The burden of guilt was gone and a peace and joy enveloped me, such as I had never known before. I went downstairs to my family expecting everyone would see the difference in me, but nothing was said. However, three days later I met two missionary ladies; Miss Marjorie Watts from the Thonon Mission and Miss Ella Colville from the Dohnavur Mission, and they asked me when I had become a Christian. I told them what had happened three days earlier and they replied, "We can see the glory all over you!" I had at last met the majestic Lord of glory, the King of Kings and the Lord of Lords.

## Born again (aged 21) 1954

*Standing alone I take my place,*
*Beneath Your cross I fall.*
*I bow to You, the God of grace*
*And give to You my ALL.*

*You died for me and suffered loss*
*Of all this world holds dear,*
*And there upon the cruel cross*
*You took my sin and fear.*

*You rescued me from death and hell;*
*You paid the ransom price*
*Of your own blood that from You fell,*
*To cleanse the grip of vice.*

*T'was Satan who had held me bound*
*For many years before,*
*But You stooped down and from the ground*
*You lifted one so poor.*

*You set me there at Your right hand*
*A Child of Yours became,*
*You gave me life, a life You planned*
*And from the King it came.*

## A New Lifestyle

CHAPTER

8

"If anyone is in Christ, he is a new creation, old things have passed away; all things have become new."
2 Corinthians 5.17

'There is an expulsive power of a new affection,' and as I had come to know and love the Lord Jesus Christ, I sensed many things were to change and had to change. From now onwards life would be very different. My first confrontation as a new Christian was with the *world*; how I would react to its demands and hostilities. The Inter Varsity Fellowship dictionary defines the world as 'society organised without reference to God, and often in opposition to Christ.' The world seems so attractive, but it is also very deceptive and I soon found that it did not satisfy my new heart's deep hunger. Indeed it became a hindrance and so I tried to steer clear of it whenever possible, and still do. Thankfully I was not told by anyone what I must or must not do in relation to worldliness and though I did not know the Bible well enough, I had an inner conviction of the Holy Spirit's guidance.

There were many society events to which I was invited and none of these were inherently wrong; the Chelsea Flower Show and Henley Regatta, which I declined to accept. I was asked to a box at The Royal Albert Hall by Otto Klemperer's wife, which I also declined, despite the fact that I adored music. It would have been wonderful to have seen the greatest German conductor of his generation, but I had lost my desire for such entertainments. They no longer held such importance in my life. I stopped going to the Medical School dances or 'hops' as they were called. Not knowing the story-line, I accepted an invitation to a play called 'The Little Hut,' which explored the relationship of a woman and two male lovers, I left in disgust. Similarly, I walked out of the film 'La Ronde.' I could not bear to see scenes of such depravity being portrayed as acceptable. I became friends with a lady called Elizabeth, the wife of the famous bassoonist Bill Waterhouse. She was a cellist and I had started to accompany her on the piano. She asked me to go and see a play with her and I agreed to go. During one particular scene a cross appeared inappropriately on the stage at an angle and I felt compelled to leave. That was the end of a friendship in its incipiency. I also stopped going to cocktail parties and drinking alcohol. People must have thought me crazy, and I am sure they did! Peter tells us in 1 Pet 4.4 "They think it strange that you do not eagerly join them … in their excesses of fun, and they heap abuse on you." As a result, I lost some friends, and I am sure I made some people very angry. The truth was that none of this worldly lifestyle fitted in with my new lifestyle. I now had a heavenly goal in my life which I had to pursue at all costs.

I certainly did not suffer any lack though, for life had become exhilarating. Instead of the boring 'jet set' life I would most surely have followed, I had the excitement of telling people about Jesus and what He had done for me. I never knew from one day to the next to whom He would lead me, what I would say, or what the reaction might be. Life was, and still is, held in enigmatic suspension waiting on the Lord's next assignment.

There were beach missions held by The Children's Special Service Mission (commonly known as the CSSM) at many seaside resorts. I helped out at the one at Bude in North Cornwall on three or four occasions and was privileged to be under the leadership of Quinton Carr, fondly known to us workers as 'Skipper.' I was usually designated to be a 'fisher,' the purpose being to collect as many children as possible to hear the gospel message. This was always delivered from a huge sand pulpit, newly erected each day and beautifully decorated with fresh flowers, pebbles, shells and seaweed. There was a verse spelled out in pebbles on the front. This is how I first learned to become a 'fisher of men,' and have been ever since. In fact it was at these beach missions that I started to fulfill the Great Commission to "Go out into the world and proclaim the gospel to everyone." Mk 16.15. This became a lifestyle that after much practice I do not find difficult; I just wait for a cue and then launch out trusting the Lord to give me the words which will be appropriate for the particular person I meet. The opportunities and openings are boundless and I wish I had taken them all.

Recently I went to see the cardiographer at my local hospital and was on the way out when a couple asked me where the cardiographer's room could be found. I told them they might easily miss it and then pointed the way including the possible false trails they could follow. While Tony went to fetch the car and bring it to the nearest exit, I waited. Lo and behold, along came this same couple and so I asked them if they had found the room easily. The man replied, " But for you and your directions we would have been utterly lost." Straight out of my mouth, not knowing they were highly educated people, (one being a lawyer who had studied at Cambridge the same time as Tony,) I said, "And I too would have been utterly lost eternally, but for someone showing me the way." I then gave them a brief resume of my testimony, to which the man listened intently. Perhaps I sowed a seed in their minds which will lead them to seek and find the Lord Jesus as their Saviour? As usual I prayed immediately afterwards and left with joy for another opening the Lord had given me. This is just an example of the way I try to grab opportunities wherever possible.

Although my new lifestyle caused some friends to drop me, I made new ones too. There were not many at first, but sufficient to help me on my way and with whom I could have fellowship; a relationship unobtainable outside the Kingdom of God. Everything had changed and I had changed; I was now seeking, or rather "hungering and thirsting after righteousness." Mat 5.6 and I was occupied with the desire to bring as many people as possible to a saving knowledge of the Lord Jesus Christ. Reinhardt Bonnke, the international evangelist's motto encouraged me, "plunder hell and populate heaven." I have led a few people to the Lord, though I wish it was more, but I have told hundreds about Him and I eagerly await to see if any are in heaven as a result.

As soon as I came to know the Lord, He revealed to me that the Bible not only contains the Word of God, but is in very essence the actual Word of God. It was not only inspired, but breathed out by holy men of God whom He chose to write it. This book therefore became my most treasured possession. Under Skipper's excellent teaching I learned the vital importance of a daily quiet time, when I could talk to God, read, mark, learn and meditate on the Scriptures. When the CSSM workers met as a team to plan the schedule, Skipper would ask us, "Have you had your two breakfasts today?" Then he would point to first his eyes and then his lips and say, "The first breakfast must be through your eyes and only then can you have the second breakfast through your mouth!" This became a habit which has been the foundation of my Christian life and my source of spiritual strength. I use Matthew Henry's commentary a great deal and write notes to help the Word of God to sink in and pray over. My motto is 'read it through, pray it in and live it out.'

In our last parish where we were for fifteen years and when the children had flown the nest, I spent much more time alone with the Lord. For three hours each morning, except Sundays, I would go up into my study and meet with Him, not knowing at first how desperately I would need this sacred time. First I read a passage of scripture, meditated on it and then wrote in my large spiritual journal. Sometimes I used the Scripture Union questions; What do I learn about God? What errors must I avoid? What commandments must I obey? and What promises can I claim? Next, I would look to see what Matthew

Henry wrote about it, underlining the important points and then I turned to praise and worship in word and song. This was followed by confession and supplication (prayer for myself) and finally I would intercede (pray for others) in a systematic and yet also spontaneous way. I learned so much in these wonderful times with the Lord, which He used later, bringing them to mind when I needed them. Nowadays I am very slowed down and take so much longer to do everything, that I only manage one and a half or occasionally two hours each morning. We rise early at 5am and have the best, most exciting, challenging and sometimes tearful part of the day alone with Jesus.

## The quiet time

*Are you waiting and longing to hear Him*
*Speak words that are needed for you?*
*Are you eagerly into the scriptures,*
*To learn and to ponder them through?*

*Do you have any time with your Saviour*
*You specially for Him set aside?*
*He will wonder if you have forgotten;*
*For you He has bled and has died.*

*Do you know the rich treasures of Scripture*
*Are better than any fine gold?*
*They are sweeter by far than the honey,*
*Its precepts your life will uphold.*

*Will you go to a room and in secret,*
*Obediently shut the door tight?*
*To commune with your Heavenly Father,*
*For He is your soul's great delight.*

*Will you choose to meet Jesus when rising?*
*Discover the change this will make,*
*For your life will be blessed beyond measure*
*If kept sacred this time when you wake.*
(References: Ps 63.1, 57.8, 90.14, Pr 8.17, Is 26.9, Mk
1.35, Luke 6.12.).

St. Paul's view towards the world is expressed in Gal 6.14,
"May I never boast, save in the Cross of our Lord Jesus
Christ, by whom the world has been crucified to me and
I to the world." How much more I need to learn, absorb
into my very being, and practice this scripture so that I
might become;

*"Dead to this world and its applause, to all its fashions, customs,*
  *laws*
*Of those that hate the humbling cross, so dead, that no desire may rise*
*To appear holy, good or wise in any but my Saviour's eyes."*
*(Author unknown)*

I long to be able to say with George Muller; *"I have died to*
*my opinions, preferences, tastes and will, died to the world's approval*
*or censure, died even to the approval or blame of family and friends,*
*and only seeking to know myself approved to God."*
   Having been made aware of the lures and dangers of
the **world,** I then had to learn how to contend with the

***devil*** and his schemes and subtleties, and to become determined to resist or flee his snares. Even when I was much older I got caught up in error, but thankfully the Lord soon rescued me out of this.

My greatest foe, however, is within; it is the ***self life***, which raises its ugly head all too often and tries to take over. This is far harder to deal with than the world or the devil. This is where the Word of God has come to my rescue. As I read it day by day it pricks my conscience, points out my sin and shows me how much my 'self' nature needs to be mortified. It reveals to me that this 'self life' has to be put back on the cross *continually*, though it screams like a pig being slaughtered. St. Paul cries out in Rom 7.24, 25 "Who can deliver me from the body of this death? I thank God, through Jesus Christ our Lord." Oh that I might so live the crucified life that I may be able to say with Paul in Gal 2.20 "I *am* crucified with Christ, and I no longer live, but Christ lives in me. The life that I now live, I live by faith in the Son of God who loved me and gave Himself for me."

## Heart transplant at the cross

*Have you been to the cross of Calvary where the glorious Son of God died?*

*Has your heart stood amazed at His meekness when your own is so ugly with pride?*

*Have you gazed at the cross and just pondered the depth of His love for you there?*

*Has your heart ever melted and broken for the pain that He bore, you to spare?*

*Have you gone to the cross for His cleansing? Have you seen your sins pierce Him right through?*

*Has your heart ached at all for its blackness? Have you realised He died there for you?*

*Have you watched as He suffered in silence for your sins that upon Him were lain?*

*Has your heart stirred at all from its deadness to the One who for you has been slain?*

*Are you washed in the blood that flowed freely that your sins might be made white as snow?*

*Has your heart been unchained from its shackles by the Saviour to all you now owe?*

*Do you come to the cross very often and with trembling kneel down at His feet?*

*Does your heart smite you ever so keenly when you wound One so gentle and sweet?*

*Have you realised the cost to your Saviour? Are you fighting the battle for Him?*

*Is your heart resolved always to stay true when it's easier to sink than to swim?*

*Are you praising the Lord for His mercy and your life's been surrendered to Him.*

*Does your heart stand amazed at His goodness for now filling your life to the brim?*

*Are you telling the world about Jesus, how He turned your life inside and out?*

*Is your heart in the great Gospel message? Will you raise your voice for Him and shout?*

*Has your life unmistakably changed, so the world means just nothing to you?*
*And your heart's being weaned from the self life through the Saviour known only to few?*

*Have you thanked the redeemer who saved you from sin's penalty, judgment and hell?*
*Is your heart now responding with ardour that with Him soon in Heaven you'll dwell?*
*Will you cling to the cross till your life's end with nothing but JESUS your goal?*
*Will your heart jump for joy when you see Him; The ONE who's enraptured your soul?*

# An unqualified Teacher

"Behold, I will do a new thing ... I will make a way in the wilderness and rivers in the desert." Isaiah 43.19

A melancholy spirit then began to envelop me, which can best be described as a sense of being in some kind of wilderness. Although the Lord had begun to revolutionise my life and had brought me into a personal relationship with Himself, my ambition to be a doctor had gone up in smoke and I was grieving its loss. I had not yet learned that my ambition must be supremely Jesus ... one goal – whatever the cost.

How would I earn a living now? I began to wonder what I might do and whether I could find something that interested me. The happiness I experienced at St. Brandon's and the adventurous spirit that had been born there and was carved deep into my subconscious, together with the Lord's guidance, led me to consider teaching as a career. I did not fancy doing any further training, but I contacted an educational agency called Gabbitas Thring, hoping that there might be a school with a vacancy for a biology teacher. It just so happened that St. Mary's Horsell, a boarding school in Woking, catering for girls between the ages of six and sixteen, desperately needed a biology teacher. They welcomed my application and accepted me immediately.

I negotiated my hours and salary having no idea what was the going rate! I soon discovered that all the other teachers 'lived-in' and were on duty for most of the time, not only for lessons. It had been agreed that I should work three days a week and stay there for the two nights in between. I was therefore working half the hours of the other teachers and as I discovered later, I was earning more than them all, despite the fact that they were trained and I was completely unqualified!

I realised that the first impression I must create in the class-room was that of being in control. Establishing a disciplined atmosphere was therefore imperative and this was not difficult with most of the classes. There was one particular class, however, who 'played-up' all the teachers and attempted to render them powerless. I was determined not to allow this to happen to me. Sure enough they were soon up to their old tricks. My first lesson began with a frog jumping out of my desk as I opened it! There was a mixture of hilarity and apprehension as they awaited my response. "I really *love* frogs," I began, "and when I was a little girl staying with my grandmother, I used to try and catch them in the recreation ground opposite her house." Their plan had fallen flat and they did not succeed in 'stealing a march' on me! The next tactic was to beam sunlight directly at my eyes. I got up nonchalantly, walked over to the child responsible (who quickly secreted the offending article into her desk) and demanded, "Open your desk and give me that mirror." As she reluctantly extracted it, I continued with a beaming smile "This is *exactly* what I want. Thank you *so* much!" The class fell silent; I resumed teaching and later gave the mirror back to the child. Never again did they try to provoke me, for I had gained their respect and could ease off with the discipline and make lessons fun and interesting.

I not only taught biology at the school, but after awhile scripture too. During breaks I found myself more drawn to be with the children than up in the staffroom. I would go into the hall where they would often congregate and start to play the grand piano, usually starting off with something flashy! There would soon be a group of children around me, and having a captured audience I could then begin to share the Gospel. The method I adopted was to switch from playing classical pieces to Scripture Union choruses, and encourage them to join in and sing. This sometimes led to a deep discussion about the Lord Jesus, during which I would open up my Bible and read an appropriate verse or two.

There was one thing I regretted during my time at this school which evoked a sense of déjà vu. There happened to be a Polish lady teaching there, who had been an inmate in the notorious 'Auschwitz' concentration camp. She was obviously deeply hurting inside, but showed little of this outwardly. I remember talking to her from time to time, but with hindsight, though I wanted to help her, what I said was probably of little or no comfort. I was now twenty two years old but still lacked the understanding, love and empathy needed. I often wonder what happened to her and whether she ever came to know Jesus as her Saviour and Healer. I was at St. Mary's for only one year as I was heading for Bible school the following academic year. Towards the end of my last term there, the head-mistress called me into her study and surprised me by saying "Miss Marcon, you are my *best* teacher!" I was amazed, but obviously greatly encouraged.

After completing Bible College, I again sought a teaching post through the same agency and received one at Stoke Poges in Buckinghamshire. At this school I did not have the same opportunities for evangelism amongst the children as I had previously. I still only worked for half the week and managed financially living at the Foreign Missions Club in Aberdeen Park, North London. Here I spent more time in the staffroom, was able to get to know the teachers better and had a chance to witness to them. One particular teacher had her class in the adjoining class-room to mine with only a thin sliding partition between the two. My class disturbed hers and vice versa, but we came to an understanding which limited the frustration. This lady was none other than the wife of the famous conductor Otto Klemperer and she very kindly took me in her car to the railway station each day. In neither of these two schools was I asked to follow a syllabus, and in both, all the girls excepting one, managed to pass their O Level Biology. This was surely a miracle!

Teaching had brought me through my wilderness experience into a new and fascinating encounter with children. The Lord in His graciousness had provided me with streams, indeed rivers, in what had become a desert.

# A surprise encounter with Prince Charming!

"...called according to His purpose." Romans 8.28

In 1955 I was living in Brighton but teaching in Woking. I attended Holland Road Baptist Church and was being prepared for believer's baptism by Pastor Rudman. His church held a missionary week each year and on the final day he asked all those who felt called to the mission field, or ministry, to come forward onto the platform. I had been sensing, ever since I came to know the Lord that He was calling me to work for Him full time. Thus I stepped forward eagerly and with alacrity, and with all the others who had responded, was encouraged by prayer.

Within a few months I was at the London Bible College. By then the 'clean air act' had come into force, so there was no longer a threat to my lungs. I opted to take the Bachelor of Divinity degree course, an absurd choice as it involved studying two foreign languages, Greek and Hebrew, both being decidedly more difficult than the English and French with which I had previously had such problems. I eventually transferred to the Certificate of Religious Knowledge which was only a one year course. I suppose I just coasted my way through the more academic subjects and never obtained any qualification, for something happened which took my full focus away from my studies! However, it was good to be there and I was blessed by the helpful teaching we received on Homiletics, (the art of preaching) Exegesis (the interpretation of a text) and the doctrine of Scripture. These have proved to be invaluable in my devotional life and my preaching ministry. Something else that came out of my time there was a friendship I struck up with Oonagh MacDonald, who later became a Member of Parliament for Thurrock. There were mostly Baptists and few Anglicans at the LBC. I was asked out by a few of the chaps, but declined. At half term I went home for the weekend and announced to my parents "I want to marry a vicar!" I had begun to feel nostalgic for the Anglican ethos of my childhood and at twenty three years old I was already beginning to feel distinctly broody!

It was February 11ᵗʰ 1957 and very warm for the time of year. On that day and for no particular reason, I took unusual care of my appearance. I wore a blue spotted cotton skirt and a white organza blouse and made an effort with my hair. I was leaving home to go back to London by train. I stepped into a carriage which only had one other occupant; a handsome young man with a 'brolly' in one hand and a book in the other. I sat in the opposite corner of the carriage and also opened up a book. As was my custom, after a little while I tried to strike up a conversation with him, hoping that it would lead to my being able to witness. My approach was audacious and one I had never used before. I simply asked him the question "Are you a Christian?" He replied "Yes" and I said "So am I." Then I asked him another question "Are you reading the Bible?" to which he again replied "Yes" and I said "So am I." Finally I ventured to ask him "Are you a theological student?" Once more he responded in the affirmative and again I said "So am I." These were honestly the only words first exchanged!

At this point, the young man came over and sat opposite me and we began to talk. He told me that he was at Oak Hill Theological College, training for the Anglican ministry and I told him that I was at the LBC. He asked me where I was living and I told him it was at the China Inland Mission. He knew of this, which later proved significant. We continued to talk all the way to London and there we parted. I had found out that he had been to Haileybury Public School, had been a commissioned officer whilst doing National Service (as my brother had) and was a Cambridge graduate from Corpus Christi. When I arrived at the China Inland Mission, I told my friend Jean Simmonds, "I've just met a super bloke in a train; he is preparing for the Anglican ministry and his name is Tony March."

"Well I never!" she replied, "That's the name of the chap who came to stay with us in Wolverhampton when my father arranged a mission in our church!" Three days later, on Valentine's Day, I received a letter from Tony asking me to an overseas student's party at his college and inviting Jean too. I showed her the letter, and her response was, "No, I don't want to be a *gooseberry*!"

I went out and bought a thick dark green silk dress for the occasion and when I arrived at the gates of Tony's college he was standing there, of course, with brolly in hand! I cannot recall very much of what happened, except discovering that he was the senior student, and having a conviction that he would one day become my husband. I invited Tony home to our vicarage in the Easter holidays and my mother's comment when he had left us was, "When you marry Tony…" I expostulated but she calmly continued, "Mother's know!" Tony invited me back to his home, which was also in Sussex, where I discovered he was the eldest of five children. I remember witnessing to his mother and not getting a very good reception!

The next important event was speech day at Oak Hill. Again I was invited and again I bought a beautiful outfit; a silvery grey and white dress in which I felt really elegant. I only mention the clothes, because until then I had never before been bothered about my appearance. Now I had a raison d'être. Tony and I were only able to see each other occasionally, but I surprised him once by turning up at a church where I heard he was preaching. He spotted me as he processed up the aisle and there was a twinkle in his eye. His sermon was on Acts 3.6; "Silver and gold have I none, but what I have I give you." It was true; Tony certainly had little of this world's goods to offer! Although I knew that Tony was the man for me, I was not in love with him. However, as his ordination drew nearer, I realised I must not miss this important occasion, in case I became his wife! Audaciously I asked him if I might come, which would involve his parents having to put me up in their hotel, taking me there and presumably paying for me and they agreed.

Tony had the privilege of being ordained at Canterbury Cathedral by the Archbishop. The famous 'Red Dean' read the scriptures beautifully. Afterwards, Tony and the other ordinands disappeared off to a retreat whilst his family and I went back to the hotel. Delicious food was laid out for us, but I could not eat, there was a comfortable bed, but I could not sleep! The weekend elapsed and I was driven home by Tony's aunt who was a warm, sweet lady with whom I found I was able to share my heart. I told her I had fallen in love with Tony and she immediately replied, "Then you must tell him, next time you meet."

When Tony next visited my flat in Swiss Cottage ... I did! Having never kissed a girl before in his life, he threw his arms around me, gave me a big bear hug that nearly squeezed the life out of me and asked, "Will you marry me?" Of course, I said I would and so we became unofficially engaged that day. I was on cloud nine! We had known each other for seven months when we became officially engaged. Knowing Tony had no money to buy me an engagement ring, his mother generously opened her box of rings and told me to select which ever one I wanted. I chose a beautiful Victorian ring with five large diamonds on the band! We had to wait a year before getting married, because the Archbishop wisely wanted Tony to have his first year of parish ministry unhindered by anything, including me. We were married exactly a year later and had hoped that this would be on September 6th 1958. However Tony's vicar had planned a holiday then and so we moved the date to September 13th.

How fortuitous this turned out to be, for on September 6th there was the biggest hailstorm ever known in the country. Hail stones the size of golf balls were recorded by the Guinness Book of Records, which smashed all the glass greenhouses in the area and flattened every flower that my father had planted especially for our wedding. This would have been disastrous for the reception was planned to be held in a marquee in the garden. Mercifully, September 13th proved to be a glorious day with the sun shining brightly! Our wedding day was not, however without its challenges. For some unknown reason, whilst my mother and sister had someone to help them get dressed, I did not. When I was finally ready to emerge and come down the stairs, everyone had already gone to the church and father stood at the bottom and roared "Hurry up or we shall be late." Then my back suddenly seized up and so I was unable to kneel during the service and we never sang our favourite hymn 'Praise, my soul," which my father forgot to announce. The final straw was when a friend of the family who gave one of the speeches did not give a very complimentary account of me, which was both surprising and hurtful. The wedding therefore proved to be rather disappointing and I was glad to escape and be alone with Tony afterwards. My mother had very kindly found and paid for a small farmhouse for us to stay at for the first weekend and that was followed by a wonderful honeymoon in Switzerland.

Five years ago our children and eight grandchildren all got together at our daughter Sarah's house, (as it is nearest to ours and because she has the largest dining table which can seat up to twenty people!) to celebrate the fiftieth anniversary of our meeting on the train. I told Tony nothing of what was going on and pretended that we were just invited over to the house for a lunch of soup and rolls. A banquet however had been prepared, and when Tony entered the dining hall he was amazed to see the table adorned with magnificent exotic flowers, a wooden track and battery powered trains running round it. Each place setting had a ticket with a name on it and each ticket bore a different destination and price dating back to 1957. There were golden balloons, serviettes and candles and a string of love hearts suspended from the balcony above us. 'Cordon bleu' food was served as well as a large cake decorated with a sugar train on top. I had written a poem reminiscing about our meeting which I read out and Tony read out a moving poem he had put in his card to me.

One year later, exactly fifty years after we married, we celebrated our Golden Wedding and arranged a special church service church to mark the occasion. I asked Sarah what she thought the theme should be and she responded instantaneously, "Well Mummy, what have you both been doing all these years?" I answered, "Proclaiming the salvation of Jesus." We agreed that this would be its essence and chose the word 'Redemption," which recalls the Old Testament practice of freeing slaves every jubilee (fifty years). Slaves were thus redeemed and we are too, by the precious blood of Christ. The service was held in a local village church. It began with our son Andrew playing the theme from 'Schindlers list' on the violin with a CD backing track. (Schindler rescued or redeemed many Jews, but Jesus redeems all who call on His Name to be saved.) In the middle of the service, our three children took leading parts; Andrew poignantly read Psalm 103, Sarah sang a solo called 'How can I be free' and Rachel gave a heartfelt reflection on childhood memories entitled "Colours of Childhood,' and followed it by reading a beautiful poem which brought tears to my eyes.

## Colours of childhood

My life began in Croydon in 1959. Most of my baby photos were in black and white and my daughter Emily, now 18 asked me when she was a small child if the world was in black and white when I was born. I thought about the question and answered that in many ways it was! Life was much more black and white then. It was only 14 years after the Second World War had ended and folk had been through an awful lot that had taught them to appreciate things that nowadays we take for granted.

But my mind is full of *coloured* threads as I think back to my childhood; all jumbled together, each one important. There is the **pink** thread of warmth and love and hugs and there were lots of these, the **yellow** thread of fun and laughter; long summer days in the garden playing badminton, building 'camps' and enjoying the company of the many friends who were always welcomed into the home, however inconvenient. Although Mum and Dad were fairly strict, they were always up for a spot of wonderfully impromptu fun! Parents who came to pick up their children in the evening would often find themselves returning home to collect pyjamas and toothbrushes so that our friends could stay for the night. I remember saying a lot of *pleases* beforehand, mind you!

Then there is the **green** thread of the appreciation of nature that was taught to us from an early age; walks in the countryside, swimming in rivers and making camp fires and cooking in the woods. The **blue** thread represents complete honesty and openness. There were no taboos and I was able to freely express my thoughts and feelings.

I also knew that I had to be willing to listen to truths about myself that were sometimes painful to hear! There was a big emphasis placed on always remaining teachable. The **purple** thread is that of warning and discipline, so vital in a child's life. I always knew the boundaries, although I was always trying to push them! One of the disciplines I was encouraged to develop was that of daily bible reading and prayer. The **orange** thread is for the glow of sibling love; we all got on incredibly well together and any scraps were very minor ones.

At four years old, influenced by my parent's faith and love for the Lord and the wonderfully clear teaching of my Sunday school teacher, Rose Reeman, I was confronted by the **black** thread of sin and the realization that I needed to be forgiven by my Saviour. I remember sitting in our breakfast room in the vicarage in London, playing a bright green 45 record on my portable record player and listening to the story of Peter Rabbit over and over again. I knew I was full of naughtiness. It was Mum who recognised what was happening in my heart and although she was initially doubtful that one so young could be aware of being a sinner, she knew that the Holy Spirit had really touched my heart. It was she who helped to lead me to the Lord, to repent of my sin and make a personal decision to follow Him. That was when I experienced the **red** thread of the cleansing power of Jesus redemptive blood which I understood so clearly, even at that very young age.

The next colour is **white**; the colour of purity and cleansing. I knew I was washed as white as snow in the blood of Jesus and that I had been forgiven and saved.

Whereas once I was a lost black sheep, now I was found and gloriously white! It was and has remained the most significant day in my life. Lastly, is the **golden** thread of love and devotion; namely that of my parent's deep love for each other. The strength of their commitment to each other and to the Lord, through thick and thin, has been a powerful influence in my life. Theirs has not been a sedentary kind of love, but an ever increasing bond and they would probably agree with me when I say that they are more in love with each other today than they were on their wedding day in 1958! What a testament their marriage and parenting skills have been to me and what a blessing it must be to the Lord.

So many memories; too many to share with you all in a 5 minute slot, but I hope this poem rounds off my thoughts today as we celebrate this special Golden Wedding Celebration.

## To my parents

*If ever a daughter was blessed, it's me. If ever a daughter was loved.*
*If ever a daughter was given the best, it was me when God gave me to you.*
*For you have been my sun and moon, the hand to guide, the warm embrace,*
*And you have been a rock to me; a voice of calm, a resting place.*
*Through all my ups and all my downs, through difficulties and pain,*
*You've been there to share my load, to pray and pray and pray again.*

*If ever a daughter was known, it's me. If ever a daughter was
    loved,*
*If ever a daughter was given the most, it was me when God gave
    me to you.*
*For you have been my sun and moon, the hand to guide, the warm
    embrace,*
*And you have been a rock to me, a voice of calm, a resting place.*

*Yes, my sun and moon and shining stars; A gift from God above.*
*How I thank Him for my parents and for their amazing love.*
*A love which first of all loves Him and that is plain to see.*
*But what a wealth of love they own, to spare so much for me.*
*Rachel Gardiner 23.06.08*

The children then sang a hymn I had written using that
old well known chorus 'In my need Jesus found me', as a
pattern. There were solos from Andrew and Sarah, an
unaccompanied verse in three part harmony and one
verse sung in unison with me playing the piano.

## In my sin Jesus sought me

*In my sin Jesus sought me, from destruction He bought me,*
*By His own blood on Calvary's cross, paid the price.*
*Loving Jesus who wooed me, matchless Saviour who won me,*
*Showed me the light, gave me the right to come to God.*

*In my mind He renewed me, placed His truth deep inside me.*
*Brought me His Word, life-saving seed; I believe.*
*Righteous Jesus who saved me, Holy One who now shows me*
*All of His ways, all of my days, I'm safe in God.*

*In my heart He transformed me, cleansed my sin He redeemed me*
*By His own blood shed on the cross; took my place.*
*Gracious Saviour who cleansed me, wondrous Spirit who filled me,*
*Took all my strife; gave me His life and peace with God.*

*In my life He has changed me, new desires placed within me,*
*Showed me His will, sovereign will; to obey.*
*Wisdom coming from heaven, blessings now to me given,*
*I'm full of praise; His Name I'll raise, my glorious Lord.*

Our friend, Steve Myall preached a moving message on Psalm 103.4 "Praise the Lord O my soul, who redeems my life from destruction." The service ended with Sarah's beautiful rendition of 'God so loved the world.' I found this service to be the most memorable and poignant I have ever attended which you may think inevitable, but many others echoed the same sentiment. A buffet reception followed at a local restaurant and Tony gave a speech which included a remark an archdeacon once made about us. "Gillian, you are the irresistible force, and Tony you are the immovable rock!" Tony placed fifty golden roses into my arms *and* the bucket of water they were in! (Which I being only six and a half stone, could not carry!) I responded with a poem I had written, thanking the Lord for such a truly wonderful and godly husband.

This is the story of how I was "called according to His purpose," both to ministry and to marriage, and certainly "All things have worked together for good." Praise the Lord!

## To my wonderful husband

*What woman ever found the man of dreams, just sitting in a
   train?*
*The one that God had planned for her, and making it so plain.*
*Most people call such meeting chance, but to this view we never
   dance,*
*For knowledge of God's sovereignty yields wealth of hope and
   certainty.*

*But yes, I've found the man God chose, more sure I am as years
   disclose*
*There could be no one else for me who'd stick so faithfully as he.*
*He vowed in poverty or wealth, in sickness or in perfect health,*
*In crisis – naught would change his heart, and he has borne the
   harder part.*

*He is my carer willingly; he does my chores so cheerfully,*
*The shopping, cleaning, gardening, my many failures pardoning.*
*A sense of humour he has brought to one in whom this gift was
   short.*
*He's full of stories, songs and jokes and roars of laughter he
   evokes.*

*He is my chaplain resident, God's will for him pre-eminent.*
*When grief and anxiousness prevail, his scriptural comforts never
   fail.*
*Yes, he's my lover and my friend; he will be with me to the end,*
*What woman ever was so blessed; for I have surely found the best.*

# For the love of children

# CHAPTER 11

"Children are a gift from the Lord." Psalm127.3

Having made pretty much of a fiasco of school, medicine and Bible College, though not teaching, thankfully, I was now determined to make a success of being a wife and mother. I put everything into this with great zeal as I had done with my medical training, and if it were possible, perhaps more. I therefore took my new role in the home as seriously as I would any other profession, needing all the skills that this would involve. How dependent I would be on the Lord's grace, wisdom and help, especially after my somewhat traumatic childhood. Starting family life with a real love for children is not only an advantage but a necessity. This love I had in great measure; fostered by my involvement with CSSM and developed during my teaching experience. Even before I met Tony I was distinctly broody, gazing through baby shop windows and pining for babies of my own!

While I was still only engaged and living at the Foreign Missions Club, there was a lovely missionary lady there called Ann Jowitt who had a pram that she no longer needed. I bought this from her and having nowhere to store it, I wheeled it through Tony's parish and deposited it at his lodgings. It did not occur to me that this might lead to the wrong conclusions being drawn, because we were both absolutely innocent. Happily, no one witnessed my 'faux pas.' This may sound unbelievable, but I can assure you that it is true; all our children were born about three weeks late, all weighed eight and a quarter pounds, all came to know and love the Lord Jesus at four years old, all are very musical and all have trained in some medical field. Two years after my daughter Rachel's conversion when she was six years old and her sister Sarah four, Rachel told her that she needed Jesus in her life. Sarah responded and Rachel led her younger sister to the Lord. When Andrew on his fourth birthday begged me to pray with him so that he too could accept Jesus into his heart, I felt it was one too much! How could all our children possibly be saved at the age of four? It was beyond my comprehension. Andrew pressed me *all* that day though, until finally worn out by his pleas and sensing that the Holy Spirit was at work, we knelt by the fire at the end of the day and he too asked Jesus to be His Saviour.

The children, however, all had very different personalities and needs. Rachel was severely dyslexic and therefore behind at school. This required extra learning help and eventually home tuition. Sarah was very bright with a particularly high IQ of 176, which made it hard to keep up with her! One day, aged only three, she put away all the weeks food shopping in exactly the right place while I was out of the room! Andrew was exceptionally musical and gifted in drama and for these he won a scholarship to prep school. In order to keep his scholarship he had to continually perform and this proved difficult because he did not have the best of health. This was the result of his having had measles at three years old when he lost half of his body weight and developed ongoing respiratory problems, from which I had to nurse him back to health many times. Throwing myself into the arena of children was a great delight, but this left me with some apprehension; I was not sure I could do any better than my mother had and worried that I might well do worse. The first grace I needed was that of unselfishness, putting my husband and my children before myself, and this I endeavoured to do. However, I did make two demands. One was that was when I entered the sitting room and one of the children was using my chair, they were to vacate it immediately without any fuss or my having to ask. The second was that I was allowed to watch one TV program a week without being bothered ... 'Panorama.' Oh how they hated it and still do!

Tony was thoroughly occupied in the parish from the moment he was ordained. He exactly followed the Church of England Prayer Book Ordinal, which states; 'Give yourself wholly to this office into which God has been pleased to call you, so that as much as lies in you, apply yourself wholly to this one thing, and draw all your cares and studies this way.' This does not exactly allow for a wife and children, so I had to be both mum and dad! Nevertheless, although obviously busy at weekends when the children were at home, Tony did spend one precious hour playing with them after they arrived home from school on Tuesdays, his day-off. As a family we always had breakfast and supper together and all meals at weekends. Here Tony proved, more than I, an expert at coaxing them to eat and he was brilliant at telling them funny stories from his vast memory store. Tony had six weeks holiday spaced over the year and these he devoted to the children. He was always a loving, understanding and gentle father. Not one sarcastic comment ever escaped his lips, or any disparaging remarks. Rather, Tony was a great encouragement to us all and an example of godly living.

There was a problem, however, and that was my lack of good health and limited physical strength which had been eroded by the effects of my motor bike accident and the London smog. These left me with musculo-skeletal problems and respiratory disorders. Tony was very understanding and helpful at these times and it was a blessing that he worked at home. I thank the Lord that I was not afflicted, as some mothers are, with serious diseases such as multiple sclerosis. I found 2 Corinthians 12.9 to be absolutely true. "My grace is sufficient for you, for my strength is made perfect in weakness." Peace in the home is what I really longed for; for myself, for my children and for Tony. One practical way of achieving this was to be organised, and this I certainly was. I performed a specific task on a specific day every week, which I maintained consistently unless circumstances dictated otherwise. I kept strictly to time, so that Tony would know exactly when the meal would be ready. The same discipline was applied to bed time and getting up in the morning. I rang a Swiss gong for meal times and expected everyone to down tools and come immediately, which they did! Of course peace is far more than organization; it is a quality that is truly from the Lord and is a great blessing to any family.

To my relief I never had any serious discipline problems. On one occasion, Andrew at the age of six was standing in the hall shortly before being taken to school and he asked me if he could get a biscuit from the kitchen. I replied "No darling," and he did not press me any further to go and get what he wanted. How thankful I was that he was an obedient child, for one minute later there was a huge crash as the lath and plaster ceiling caved in. Huge pieces, some as big as quarter of a hundred weight fell and Andrew was spared from serious hurt or even worse.

As with most other mothers, I was kept busy ferrying children to their three separate schools and as they grew older, to many extra mural activities. Looking back perhaps I pressed them too hard and did not give them sufficient time to relax, or space just to be themselves. Besides this, there were church duties; meetings to attend, door and phone bells to answer and needy people to be counselled and loved. If there was a clash of loyalties, however, I always put the children before the parish. I do not regret this in any way. Meals were special times; they were usually in the kitchen on an enormous melamine table that had to be built in-situ which was useful when we had students living with us. All meals in the kitchen were called 'Pig's Meals.' Here the children were allowed, within reason, to behave more or less as they wanted and have fun. When we had formal meals in the dining room it was a very different matter. These meals were called 'Queen's Meals' when the silver, the cut glass tumblers and the serviettes would come out. Here the children's behaviour had to be impeccable and as they grew older, were encouraged to serve us rather than vice versa. On special occasions the children would prepare us a banquet, with the menu being kept a close secret.

On Saturday morning I gave the children domestic science lessons and taught them how to wash, iron, mend and cook and so on. Eventually they surpassed my feeble efforts and I learned from them, which I still do! This was especially helpful when I was in bed for weeks with back trouble and they were able to cope wonderfully. We were blessed with a very large and beautiful vicarage while the children were growing up. The huge main bedroom was turned into a play room which gradually over the years became stacked with every imaginable toy that a child could want, usually having been given by grandparents or aunts. The play room sometimes became a 'village;' Tony's childhood Hornby train track was set up in the middle and all the rest of the village was arranged round it. This consisted of a railway station, a church made out of wooden bricks or Lego, a farmyard, a kit garden, a dolls house and anything else they could incorporate! These would stay in place for several weeks until the room had to be cleaned, when everything was then moved back to the walls along with the other toys. In the centre of the room, hanging from a beam was a trapeze-cum-swing, which proved to be a very popular attraction for the children's friends.

We were also blessed with a large garden, full of activities for children. Here too I loved to join them in their games or sit on the veranda and watch them. I also enjoyed dancing with the children; we would push back all the furniture in our large sitting room, put on a record such as 'The Sound of Music' and dance, I fervently singing "I've got *confidence* in me!" I wondered if I had enough, but I knew my confidence must be in the Lord. I would spend an hour each day playing with the children or watching them play. On Saturdays we would sometimes go to Frant Wood; collect branches and twigs, light a fire in a clearing and cook a fry up, or we would go off for a walk and bathe in a river. Other times I would take the children to Tonbridge open air pool, very early in the morning before school, have a swim and then serve a hot breakfast from thermos flasks to warm us all up. The children played well together and if they quarrelled, which was rare, I sent them *all* to their own bedrooms to cool off. If I was not present when the disagreement happened, I could not possibly know who the culprit was, so I never blamed any of them! After a short while I would let them come back to play together and happiness reigned. This was a good policy as there might have been a parishioner downstairs with Tony and we all needed to be a good witness.

We found it quite hard to make 'ends meet' on a vicar's salary, with such a large house to furnish and maintain, plus the three children. I devised all sorts of methods to keep the ship afloat, especially in the 1970's when inflation was running at twenty six percent. Sarah, whose school friend's parents ran a pub, would collect the fresh crusts that were normally thrown out to the birds in the park behind. Tony and I would eat these with marmite for lunch. We turned off the central heating until clothes in cupboards became mouldy. The hot water system was only turned on for washing clothes and we filled up the bath once a week. The rest of the time we washed up and washed ourselves using kettles of boiling water. Often the children had second hand clothes and they wrapped themselves in a blanket when doing homework. All food was strictly weighed out and costly outings such as going to the cinema became impossible.

Occasionally I used to get angry, though this was not normally aimed at the children. Once, however I became furious with Rachel, and hit her with a tennis racket in its wooden press; she grabbed the curtains to try to steady herself and the curtains and rod came crashing down. Years later I had to ask her forgiveness. I never shouted at the children, rather the opposite, I would lower my voice to a whisper and point my finger, and then they knew I meant *business*! It was poor Tony who got the sharp edge of my tongue and became the scapegoat for my frustration. When the pressure seemed too great, I would shut the windows, so the neighbours might not hear. This may sound dreadful, but we were living very much in the public gaze, under scrutiny and people's expectations are sometimes unrealistic. I therefore had to be very careful not to be a stumbling block to anyone.

Family prayers featured regularly and we often had these sitting round the kitchen table. Andrew as a toddler would try and disrupt us by crawling under the table. One night he saw an angel and from that moment onward he was as good as the girls. I do not know what actually transpired, but it was sufficiently dramatic to bring about this change. Actually, I only had to reprimand Andrew severely three times during his childhood because he truly was an angelic child. Sarah was very self contained and sensible and caused me no problems, but Rachel, being the eldest and the one on whom I learned my parenting skills, was wrapped over the knuckles many times. On one occasion she swore at me and I put soap on her tongue to stop this immediately. No one else ever swore in my presence. Each night I would read to the children and pray with them individually. Each morning I would go into their bedrooms, close the window, give them a drink of Ribena and then put their Bible and Scripture Union notes into their hands. Thus they established a habit which they have maintained ever since.

I used to count the years we had left with our children at home and dreaded the day when they would leave the nest. If only life could go on like this for *ever*, I used to catch myself thinking! When they had all eventually left I was devastated as I walked past empty bedrooms. At first a sadness fell upon me like an unwelcome shroud. I had not imagined how empty our home would feel without the children, and I missed them so much. I missed their laughter. I missed their noise. I missed them so terribly. It was then that the Lord opened up another sphere for me; full time Christian work in our church and outside too, and I became totally reconciled to the fact that the children had flown.

We thank the Lord with all out hearts that all our children love the Lord, we pray that they may continue to grow in grace and in the knowledge of Him and that "The things of earth will grow strangely dim, in the light of His glory and grace." I wrote this poem many years later on reflection.

## How good to be at home

*How good to be at home, my own sweet home,*
*Although it's great to spread my wings and roam.*
*There's nowhere rivals here on earth, the peace*
*My home provides. Old memories never cease*
*To delight a heart so filled with gladness,*
*While yet other memories, tinged with sadness*
*Blend, to heighten shades of life's blessed contrast –*
*Creating thankfulness within, held fast.*

*How good to be at home in my own space*
*While world that rushes by at frightening pace*
*Is shut awhile outside, and out of mind,*
*A world that is not always tender, kind.*
*I sit in flower decked garden deep in thought,*
*And ponder … joys and sorrows life has brought,*
*Old memories welling up with mingled tears,*
*One day to fill a bottle made past years.*

*How good my heart to heavenly home is drawn*
*Where all God's precious promises will dawn.*
*What joys await me there? What sorrows bought*
*My soul from death? This soul my Saviour sought*
*And rescued out of hell's dread grasp; to keep*
*For ever by His grace and so to reap*
*A special blessing that is His to give;*
*A heavenly home, a better home, to live.*

# The challenge of Dyslexia

"Counsel is Mine and sound wisdom. I am under-standing" Proverbs 8.14

There came a time when I was having minor problems with rebellion in our eldest child, Rachel. I longed to counsel and help her to surmount this problem, but the more I said, the worse she became. So I asked the Lord what I should do. I asked for His wisdom, and He showed me through the saga of a Busy Lizzie. At that time I had a very large and beautiful Busy Lizzie, covered in pink flowers which I kept on my piano. I remember one day someone remarking how lovely it was and yet by the very next day it had unaccountably started to wither. I was really disappointed, but assuming it must be dry, I doused it with water, but to no avail … it went flop! Then I sprayed it with insecticide, but still there was no recovery. Finally I applied some plant food, but it shriveled up and seemed to be dead. I put it in the garage to throw out later and forgot all about it for awhile. When I eventually remembered and came to throw it away, to my surprise and delight, this Busy Lizzie was not dead at all, but very much alive!

Then the Lord reminded me of my request concerning

Rachel and He said to me, "That is how I want you to deal with Rachel; do not say anything, do not do anything, just leave it all to Me. When you watered the plant it withered and died, but when you left it alone it began to flourish." I took the plant back up to the sitting room and thought I would put just *one* egg cup full of water on it. I did, and immediately it wilted again. The Lord then said to me "No, not even one egg cup full of advice must you give Rachel or she will wilt and die."

I really needed wisdom when Rachel at six years old was having big problems at school which were not understood by the teachers or by us. She was being bullied by the girls and even by her class teacher for being stupid and she became very unhappy. Describing it later, she wrote; "School was hell!" and drew a picture depicting the dislike and disdain she had then felt from the teachers and children. To compound the situation, her sister Sarah at two years her junior, was reading and writing at the age of three. At that stage we had no idea that Sarah's IQ was well above Mensa, and no idea that Rachel had severe dyslexia, a condition that was not recognised in the 1960's because its diagnosis and treatment was only in its incipiency. Dyslexia is hard to diagnose and hard to define and I had to do a lot of research to discover the salient features, the effects on the child and the remedies needed. It is a specific learning disorder, affecting reading writing and spelling. It used to be known as 'Word Blindness.'

The first thing we noticed in Rachel was clumsiness and an inability when in a dancing class to know which was her right or left foot. She found it difficult to catch a ball, she was often left out when a sports team was selected and she was not reading or writing like all the other children in her year. Therefore, not only was Rachel's education adversely affected because she could not keep up with the others in her class, but her relationships with the children and her teachers were impoverished due to lack of understanding. This in turn affected her emotionally, causing her stress and a sense of failure. Looking back, considering where she is now, this was so sad because Rachel was not only intelligent, but also very imaginative, creative and musical. It obviously must have spoilt some of the joys of childhood, although she often tells me how happy she was at home. She is quick to remember the good things and slow to remember the bad things in her life, which I am sure has helped her greatly.

When it became all too apparent that something was seriously upsetting Rachel's education, I took her to see Dr. Critchley, who was a pioneer in the field of dyslexia, at the National Hospital in Queen's Square, London, and he diagnosed Developmental Dyslexia. We then took her out of her school and even moved right away to another parish which was in Tunbridge Wells in order to be near a school that we thought would help. It became clear after awhile that the school's whole educational ethos was underpinned by the occult and so we had to remove her. From there she went to several other schools, all with no success and further stress. Eventually I talked to the senior Educational Psychologist in London, who happened to be living in our road and was the secretary of our parochial church council. Without hesitation he advised that Rachel be withdrawn form ordinary schooling and be given private tuition at home instead. For me the problems were fourfold; would Tony agree to this crazy idea, how would we finance this venture, for we certainly did not have the means to do so, how would we find suitable competent teachers and would the Education Authority agree? There were mountains to overcome and the whole prospect was daunting.

The first mountain was overcome when Tony agreed to the project. This was remarkable because he is slow to make decisions in order to get them right. He also tends to be very conservative in his approach, so that doing anything as rash as taking a child out of the education system would normally have been unthinkable. However, Tony felt Rachel's unhappiness deeply. He also knew that I had the bit between my teeth and that it would not be wise to stand in my way!

Tony and I began to discuss the possibilities and pray for wisdom and guidance. The second mountain was climbed when an educational trust was established by one of my great aunts, called the Dallas Smith Trust. It came into existence at exactly the moment we needed it and we were promised that all the fees would be provided. The third mountain, to our amazement was easily overcome, for our Sunday School Superintendent, Betty MacIldowie, agreed to take on the vast majority of Rachel's tuition. It was the fourth mountain that proved to be the most time consuming. I had to draw up a carefully planned programme and time table, and then a curriculum and a general syllabus of studies. Having done this, I submitted my plan to the Kent Educational Committee and received a personal visit from their Educational Psychologist. They accepted it and we began to get everything ready in earnest. Before I explain this plan, I must tell you of a further and wonderful provision of the Lord, which proved extremely important. It just so happened that Rachel's best friend, Melinda, was also very unhappy at school. After discussing the situation with us, her parents agreed that she should join Rachel with private tuition, thereby avoiding the danger of isolation, which would have been detrimental. They spent three happy years together under this scheme, bouncing ideas off one another and fostering a healthy element of competition in their studies.

I then set about establishing a small school of just two pupils, with myself as the headmistress! It involved some hard thinking and the re-arrangement of my usual schedule. I drew up a more specific syllabus and a time table, procured certain essential equipment and more importantly sought suitable teachers to cover the subjects that were beyond Betty's remit. To begin with, I taught Melinda and Rachel Biology and Domestic Science, but later on I found an excellent Biology teacher called Dr Dence. It must be noted that what I did back then in the 1970's was very avant-garde and unusual and I had never been trained as a teacher. What I realised was the necessity of providing a balanced education; the academic, the cultural, the physical, together with social integration. All had to feature in the right proportions.

The Lord greatly blessed us with Betty, an extraordinarily able, well educated and gracious lady. She taught the girls the vast majority of the academic subjects; English Language, English Literature, History, Geography, French, German and Book Keeping. The curate at

St. John's church taught Scripture. Cultural subjects were right up Rachel's street; she was already proving to be gifted with art, music and drama. We were able to find teachers for drama and elocution, guitar, piano and singing and on Saturday mornings, she and Melinda attended the Adult Education Centre for art lessons. Physical activity was partly supplied by ballet, tap and modern dancing lessons at the Miss Conibear's School of Dancing and she also joined the tennis club, had riding lessons and swam at the Monson Road Swimming Baths. At home there was badminton, table tennis and 'Padda' tennis and Rachel cycled everywhere, covering up to twelve miles each day going from one tutor to the next.

The most important need now was for social integration with other children which she derived from her involvement with the Guides, the Sunday school, the Youth Fellowship, art classes and the ballet school. By far the most significant need was met in her relationship with Melinda, a child of her own age and without whom life would have been very different and seriously lacking. The vicarage already contained much of the equipment we needed, including a large bookcase with a wide selection of books, especially classics, suitable for children of all ages. It had a large garden where the girls could exercise and have fun together. There was a room set up with table tennis and another for billiards, the piano to play and many other musical instruments available. We had already built up a sizable collection of art and craft materials and there was an easel and paints and so on.

I then turned my attention to Rachel's bedroom which also became her school room. I gave her a bureau and made sure there was adequate lighting. I wrote down on a large sheet of cardboard all the do's and don'ts to look at and apply every time she wrote anything and she duly followed this advice. Next on the list was the timetable. Every morning started with music practice, as a fresh mind was needed for sight reading which she found particularly difficult. This was followed by three hours of homework in different subjects, and a break for coffee. Our Swiss gong was rung when it was time to change subjects! In the afternoons Rachel cycled off to her various tutors and usually in the evenings she mixed with other children to have that essential contact.

The Educational Psychologist came three times the first term, once the next and then never again during the remaining three years of private tuition. I met him accidentally just after Rachel had finished her O Levels and I asked him why he had never returned. He told me that there was no need to because he had never before in his life seen such excellent home tuition. I then ventured to ask him the results of Rachel's IQ test that he had taken before the private tuition began. He told me that he could not really divulge this information, but I tentatively asked him if was above the average of 100? It was. Was it above 110? He nodded. Then I went up to 120 and again he nodded. Finally and hesitatingly I asked him, while pointing out that this was my last question, was it over 130. He could not contain himself any longer and said loudly, "Yes!" I did not press him any further but I still wonder today if Rachel's intelligence might have been as high as 140, for, had that been the case she would have a Mensa brain too!

Rachel took seven O'Levels at just under sixteen and passed five of them. She failed French completely by walking out of the exam and for some unknown reason she also failed History, her favourite subject. At sixteen, Rachel began to train as a Nursery Nurse at West Kent College, having turned down a place at grammar school to do A Levels. Afterwards she trained as a nurse at the Kent and Sussex and Pembury Hospitals. She finally went to train as a PA secretary at the Brighton Technical College, but she became engaged and quit the course, much to the consternation of the college who said she was their best PA pupil. Since then Rachel has developed many skills, including running a large play group and helping to organize a monthly children's service in an Anglican Church for a six year period. Here she was able to utilize her music, drama and art as well as giving talks. She was once asked by the vicar whether she had thought of applying as a lay reader or going into the ministry!

Rachel has become a wonderful counsellor to needy people, but most of all she has developed into a vivacious, scintillating, delightful and compassionate person, with an exceptionally lovely character. Above all, she brings to everyone, wherever she goes, the sweet fragrance of Jesus Christ. We praise God for this wonderful gift of our daughter Rachel, for His amazing provisions for her, and the way He has used her difficulties, weaving them into the beautiful pattern we can all see. This poem exactly describes her.

## Joyful Spirit

*This joyful spirit none can quell*
*Through thick and thin her laugher rings*
*Surmounting obstacles that spell*
*Disaster; yet from her there springs*
*An ever flowing merry well*
*Of happiness; to all she brings*
*The sweetness of a perfumed dell*
*Of flowers; like nightingale she sings*
*The songs of love; she wants to tell*
*The world of One to whom she clings.*

# Miracles galore

# CHAPTER 13

"In the last days, God says, 'I will pour out My Spirit'"
Acts 2.17

I was at the stage when I had three young children.
Andrew was only a few months old and I was suffering
with post natal depression following his birth, which
continued for a whole year. However the Lord spoke to
me at this time, through John 16.24 and said "You have
not asked me about this, now *ask*, that you may receive
and have real *joy*." I believed and held on to this scripture
for another six months until one day I noticed that the
depression had vanished. During this period of time I
needed surgery; a submucous resection to correct a
problem in my nose. It just so happened that both Rachel
and Sarah were booked into the Whittington hospital for
tonsillectomies at exactly the same time as my operation,
and in the same wing. This was a real blessing as I was
able to visit the children frequently. We all returned home
together, but I was left trying to nurse myself and the children back to health, care for a baby and run the home.
This took its toll on me, I developed pneumonia and soon
after this, a nasty condition called erythema nodosum,
which required bed rest.

I had now been a Christian for twelve years, and one day while I was still unwell, the Reverend David Watson came to see us. He and Tony belonged to a rather august society called 'Eclectics.' David sat on the end of my bed and talked to me about the Holy Spirit and what He was doing afresh. I felt as if Jesus Himself had visited me and as a result I attended a meeting in connection with this. It was not until a little later, while I was on my knees praying that I asked the Lord to "Fill me with all the fullness of the Godhead bodily." Col 2.9. Paul prayed this prayer, so why shouldn't I? After all, Paul told us to be imitators of him as he was of Christ. Immediately I prayed this Scripture, these words came out of my mouth – "Elkanah Adaiah Note" It sounded like Hebrew, so I looked up in Young's concordance to try and discover what it meant. Being fairly confident that it was not 'gobbledygook,' I rang up the local Jewish Rabbi, who like my husband, was a chaplain at the Whittington hospital. When I told him what was coming out of my mouth, he exclaimed, "Oh that this could happen to me! … The Lord is possessing you" and I replied "And he can fill you too. It is prophesied in Joel."

This was a watershed in my life and I was literally on fire for the Lord. He put fire in my bones and fire in my mouth. John the Baptist said in Luke 3.16 "He (Jesus) will baptise you with the Holy Spirit and with fire." The Lord had visited me with His Holy Spirit in a fresh new way, and I was able to hear Him speak more clearly and more directly into my heart, as well as through the Scriptures and I began to move in the gifts of the Holy Spirit.

## God's Fire

*O make my heart with passion burn,*
*From any coldness may I turn.*
*Luke warmness hate and ever spurn,*
*And from Your passion let me learn.*

*Put coals of fire on worthless deeds,*
*To burn away the rotten seeds*
*Of apathy, and all that needs*
*Refining, which Your Life impedes.*

*You plucked me from the burning fire.*
*You pulled me from the pit of mire.*
*A fate so horrible, so dire,*
*My heart, my life, my all require.*

*O kindle me with Holy Flame,*
*With zeal and love may I proclaim*
*My Lord and Saviour's glorious Name,*
*That I, through You, the lost reclaim.*

*Now make my heart a living fire;*
*From ceaseless worship never tire.*
*My whole life give to You, entire,*
*And You alone be my desire.*

*So may my heart with passion strong*
*Burn every day and all day long.*
*My fervent praise and heartfelt song*
*To You, the God of fire, belong.*

One Sunday afternoon, a few days after uttering this short Hebrew tongue, I was travelling by train to see the Reverend Michael Harper and had just walked onto an escalator. Suddenly I heard a voice booming behind me; that of a black man. When I reached the top I paused and asked him who he was and he told me his name was Sid, and that he had been sitting behind me in church that morning. Then, these words came straight out of my mouth. "Stop, do not go where you are going." In my mind's eye I could see Sid turning right outside Euston Station and then turning right again and into the house of a prostitute. "Get right with the Lord, get back to Him now." I continued urgently. With that he left politely. It was not until three months later that Sid and his wife turned up at the vicarage door. Tony took Sid into one room and I took his wife into another and asked her what the problem was. She told me that Sid was involved with a prostitute in Euston and that it was wrecking their marriage.

Another clear word of knowledge came to me when two young foreign students arrived at the front door one day. They wanted to know what the teaching of the Church of England was. Tony was out at the time, so I very briefly explained and then gently introduced them to the gospel we proclaimed. They listened attentively and then one of the girls expressed anxiety that she had lost her bag containing her passport, flight tickets and money. In my mind's eye I could immediately see a restaurant with a wooden cartwheel, tables and chairs outside, with people eating and drinking and a bag lying on the ground. I saw someone pick it up and take it away. I did not tell the students what I had seen, but I did tell them that I felt it had been stolen and so I said, "Let's pray." We bowed our heads and I prayed, "Lord God, may the thief who has stolen the bag be so convicted of this crime that it becomes too hot to handle and be compelled to return it." Since the students were due to leave Britain the next day I said to them; "Please let your landlady know when you've retrieved your bag and ask her to ring and tell me?" Then I continued "Oh, and by the way, you will find your bag exactly where you left it at that restaurant with the wheel." A little while later their landlady rang me to tell me that this is exactly what happened!

Another direct word of knowledge came when I was making Andrew's bed one morning. I could see boys throwing compasses in his classroom at school. I quickly knelt down by his bed and beseeched the Lord to put a stop to this dangerous prank immediately. When Andrew arrived home, knowing that I was very fussy about any harm coming to people's eyes, he said to me, "You will never guess what was going on in my classroom today!" I replied, "No I won't guess, I'll tell you ... the boys were throwing compasses weren't they. Was anyone hurt?" He was absolutely amazed and he assured me no one was injured. I told him what I had seen that morning and that I had prayed earnestly that the Lord would intervene. Praise God, He did!

Occasionally the Lord gave me a word of knowledge through a dream at night. I once dreamed I was taking Andrew to his preparatory school, when the car mysteriously veered dangerously off the road, and down a steep embankment. I woke up sensing that the Lord was trying to warn me, and decided that I must drive very slowly round this particular corner on my journey to school. I drove very carefully indeed; nevertheless the car was inexplicably drawn towards the slope, and I could barely keep the car on the road. When I reached the school, two masters greeted me in the drive with "Do you know that your front tyre is completely flat?"

Another dream the Lord gave me was that of a tea party at which Richard and Sabina Wurmbrand were speaking. Richard had been the head of the Lutheran Church in Romania and had languished in prison for fourteen years, for the love of His Saviour. I was present, and the proceedings started with our forming a circle, so that the Wurmbrands could shake each guest's hand. When they came to me they kissed me. A while after this I received an invitation to one such tea party and indeed the Wurmbrands were present! There were other guests there too and as in my dream we formed not a full, but a semi circle. Richard and Sabina went around shaking hands with each one until they came to me. They kissed me and whispered "You are going to suffer." How right they were, because in a relatively short space of time, suffering, the gravity of which we had never experienced before, began. You can see that the word of knowledge that the Lord gave to me, prepared me to receive the word of knowledge that God gave through the Wurmbrands.

One night I had a dream that I was in a university where I was preaching to students in a round room. I had never really been a speaker before, although I had been asked to very occasionally and always felt that my attempts were rather pathetic. Nevertheless, I felt the Lord's hand on me and so I prepared a message on intercession. Soon after this, a member of the university Christian Union committee came to the vicarage. I remember that Tony and I were together in the kitchen. This young man told us there was to be a mission at his university in two weeks time, but that the person chosen to give the preparatory talk beforehand was unfortunately indisposed and unable to come. He asked Tony if he could fill the gap. Immediately I said "Please excuse me, but it's not Tony, it's me!" He looked somewhat taken aback at my forthrightness, but I told him about my dream and I asked him what was to be the subject of the talk. "Intercession," he replied, "Then it is definitely me!" I expostulated. "I've already prepared a message on intercession."

The young man told us that they had never had a female speaker before, to which I replied, "Well, there is always a first time!" He agreed to go and ask the committee what they felt, and a day of so later he told me "You're on!" I now began to feel nervous. What had I let myself in for? I polished up my talk, took my tape recorder along with me and there it was, the Round House at Sussex University, where the Christian Union met! I spoke for an hour with unusual ease as the Lord put words into my mouth. The students were on the edge of their seats; sometimes quiet, sometimes with tears and sometimes laughing at the way I put things. I was invited back to speak at other university Christian Unions in the South East. I was now more able to help with the messages needed for our large youth fellowship which gathered at the vicarage every Sunday evening. It had grown from two to about fifty members and there was barely any space on the sitting room floor. I also began to preach in church and was always meticulous about preparation. Thus was born a preaching ministry which would not have been possible except through the prompting and power of the Holy Spirit.

When Andrew was seventeen, he had mumps which developed into orchitis. The doctor visited him and prescribed the appropriate medication. Every evening his temperature rose by about two degrees Fahrenheit and one morning was up to 103°F. I believe he had developed meningitis, for as the day wore on, his temperature shot up alarmingly to 105°F and nothing seemed to help to bring it down. It happened that another vicar's wife phoned me that day and I briefly told her about Andrew's condition. She asked me if I knew about the story of Achan in Joshua 7.11 "The children of Israel transgressed God's law and took the *accursed thing* ... and put it amongst their own possessions." I said I did not know this story. We had Jackie Pullinger's niece staying with us at the time and she seemed to know all about this sort of thing. She said, "Let's go round the house and see if the Lord will show us anything He doesn't want here." We hunted everywhere. There were some African objects, some Indian snake shaped candle sticks and several books in which were signs of the zodiac. In fact we found quite a lot of things that I had no idea had any occult connection hidden somewhere within. We filled up two black bin liners and dumped them by the outside bins. This took about two hours. When I returned to take Andrew's temperature it was 99°F, praise the Lord. This was His supernatural healing which might also be called a house cleansing. I believe the

Lord wanted me to be obedient to Him and get rid of some of the possessions I treasured that did not honour Him.

I must still have treasured earthly things too much however, because a strange thing happened recently; I was reading Heb 10, when verse 34 hit me, "You … joyfully accepted the spoiling of your goods." My mind went back to the many occasions we hosted meetings in our home and when sometimes things were broken or damaged. For example, when our complete set of valuable, good reproduction Sheraton chairs was vastly devalued by a very rotund lady who sat on one and reduced it to firewood! Inwardly I would get upset and annoyed, but now the Lord was convicting me and I repented with tears. We were about to have lunch on the patio and I noticed a large, mauve bird dropping on one of our new cushions. I went to get something to remove the stain but on my return I could find no trace of it at all. We looked at each cushion, turning them over to make sure, but still no stain was to be found. We were amazed! Then the Lord showed me that He had indeed removed the stain of my propensity to desire everything to be perfect in my home and He chose to do this in a miraculous way.

There have been several people on whom I have laid hands that have been healed. The first was an almost totally blind Jewish lady called Mrs. Rappaport. She worked for the BBC and came back to our vicarage, thrilled at what God had done for her in restoring her sight. The next was Carol Cunningham-Woods. I was at a meeting when suddenly the speaker pointed to me and said, "Yes, you, turn round and pray for the woman behind you who has a problem." I wanted to fall through the floor, but reluctantly submitted to the speaker's request. It was my friend Carol, the founder of our children's play group, called 'Little Fishes.' She told me about her heart problem and I duly prayed for her. She never suffered from this condition again! Then there was Rosemary who had seriously hurt her spine when using a water slide in a swimming pool. She suffered dreadfully and the hospital exacerbated the problem when they tried to alleviate the pain. Thankfully, she was eventually allowed to receive the Disability Living Allowance which proved to be of great benefit, as her family was not at all well off. I spent quite a lot of time with Rosemary over the years, often praying with her or in some way seeking to encourage her. For several years however, I had no direct guidance to pray with her for her physical healing. One day Rosemary asked me and another church member to come and see her, which we duly did. We talked together for a while and then I felt the Lord telling me, "Go and lay hands on Rosemary." So I went and put my hands on her back and simply said, "In the Name of Jesus be healed." Graciously the Lord healed her and being an honest woman she handed back her DLA, and has, to my knowledge, never had this problem again.

Our daughter Sarah, by this time married, had a gardener called Eric Hitchman, who lived next door to her. One day Eric suffered a severe stroke and a heart attack in the car park along the Pembury Road in Tunbridge Wells. It was the day of the annual carnival and so the ambulance had trouble getting to him as quickly as it normally would. Eric lay there without any medical help for half an hour. Eventually he was picked up and taken to hospital where he was placed in intensive care. Sarah rang to tell me this and so I went directly to the hospital, taking with me our friend, John McGowan. Eric was near to death when we arrived and breathing with that characteristic 'death rattle' sound. We spent quite a long time praying for him, until we noticed that his breathing had changed. We immediately told the sister and waited outside the ward while she went in to see him. "He's turned the corner" she exclaimed as she came back out. Eric was finally able to leave hospital and return home, with only a weakness in one hand.

I will end the chapter with one bona fide miracle. It was Ivy, our church cleaner who arrived at our vicarage one day and said, "My feet are hurting so badly and I've not been able to wear shoes for years because my feet are so arthritic. All I can wear are these slippers." I asked if I might pray for her and she agreed. I bent down, put my hands on her feet and said "Ivy, be healed in the Name of the Lord Jesus Christ." She left and I did not see her for a week. That particular week had been the one before Sarah's wedding and so I had 'closed up shop' and turned off the phone and door bells. After the wedding Ivy arrived at our front door and exclaimed, "I've been trying to get hold of you for a whole week since you prayed for me. Just look, I'm now wearing shoes for the first time in years because I've got new feet, just like babies' feet!" How great is our God! He is "The same yesterday, today and forever." Heb 13. 8.

Praise God He has not changed, nor ever will – and the gifts of the Holy Spirit have not ceased. In fact they are mentioned in several places in the New Testament. (See 1 Cor 12, Eph 4.7–12, Rom 12.3–8, Heb 2.4, 1 Pet 4.7–11 and all over Acts.) I feel strongly that unless we use scissors to cut out these passages, which we are strongly warned not to do in Rev 22.19, we cannot escape their continued existence. I can find nowhere in Scripture that declares that the gifts have ceased. My certainty that this is the truth has been reinforced by the many wonderful works that the Lord God Almighty has wrought in my life and in others… too many to recount. The Lord bestows these gifts on us His children both for our own personal good and for the good of the body of Christ. So, let us not be afraid, but welcome them with open arms, for then we will see how wonderfully generous and kind is our heavenly Father.

# Caught up in deception

"Be careful that no man deceives you." Matthew 24.4

Some time after experiencing the gifts of God's Holy Spirit, this is exactly what happened to me. I was caught up in the deception of the enemy through a man, for the enemy is so subtle and persuasive in twisting the truth.

I attended the conference of a well known American preacher in 1993, having no expectation or knowledge of the man. During one of the sessions we were asked to go forward to receive prayer for gifts of the Holy Spirit and then lay hands on someone else. I did so and as I laid my hands on the nearest person, I slumped to the floor where I lay for what seemed hours, rolling around and gripped by uncontrollable laughter. I arose so 'drunk' that I could not walk a straight line for several days. I was convinced that God had dramatically touched my life, healing me physically, emotionally and spiritually. People there from a well known church had never seen anything like it before and they felt that God was preparing me for unique service.

However, after a few months, what I was told was a *special anointing from God*, had evaporated with all its alleged benefits. I spoke to a godly man about this and he correctly pointed out the Scripture in 1 John 2.27 "The anointing which you have received of Him abides in you." Why then did I feel such loss, and why was the joy now replaced with a sinister sense of foreboding? Holy Spirit gifts are always good gifts and what I was experiencing definitely was not. I therefore began to realise that this so called 'anointing' had come not from the person of the Holy Spirit at all, but from an alien spirit emanating from a false messiah under whose influence I had fallen. What I thought I had lost I had actually gained; a foothold for the enemy, and this was something from which I needed to be freed and was a few months later.

At this time a new phenomenon which had not yet surfaced in Britain, burst in upon the church and to my knowledge I was alone in this *experience*. I had therefore personally to learn the old truths all over again, slowly and painfully, that "Godliness ...which is such great gain," (1 Tim 6,6) does not come easily. It is a hard slog with full glory only at the end. It is on our knees, with tears, with the Word of God and with consistent discipline, that right-eousness and holiness are imparted. It is not a sudden zap and there are no short cuts. It is a walk by faith, when sometimes God even seems to withdraw Himself and the consciousness of His sweet presence is strangely missing. This is what saints like John of the Cross, Madam Guyon and Job discovered.

At around the time I had become aware of the false-hood of this movement amongst charismatics, I happened to break a tendon in my knee which grounded me for three months. I utilized this time by discovering all I could about this phenomenon and the Scriptural counter-arguments. I wrote an article for a Christian magazine which became the thesis for my Lay Readership. Eventually an audio tape was made of it and it was circulated. This is the essence of what I learned and passed on.

There are many different manifestations reported by people from varying theological backgrounds and fellowships. It seems unusual for all the phenomena to appear in one congregation. Many are lulled into a false sense of security by the absence of the more controversial manifestations in their own particular fellowship. There are bizarre manifestations such as animal noises; growling, roaring or sounding like a chicken, hysterical or mocking laughter, drunkenness, falling backwards and being unable to get up, jerking, violent shaking, levitation (a form of witchcraft which is strictly forbidden by God. Deut 18.10, 11) and fanning to direct the wind of the Spirit and blowing on the congregation so that they fall under the power.

The Charismatic Renewal has been infiltrated with New Age philosophies, with an admixture of both psychological and demonic factors emerging. Some features that worried me were the hype, the ear splitting levels of music with its heavy and mesmeric beat resembling pagan chants. Another concern was the careful psychological preparation of the meeting by *expectancy*, which is actually auto-suggestion. For instance a space is cleared, people are told what will happen and then they are asked to 'wait on the Spirit' whilst standing for lengthy periods of time, so that manifestations are bound to appear. There is the use of hypnotism, though not recognised, when people are so-called 'slain in the Spirit' and fall backwards, passing out in a semi- conscious state. Manipulation is used to evoke a response. Group dynamics play a large part in this modern cult. Hedonism can be observed; pleasure seeking, the source of pleasure not in this case being derived from the world, but from the church setting. There is a dependence on feelings and emotions which are then exploited. Finally I noticed the apparent necessity for instant solutions. The idea being, it is easy if you have that *special* knowledge and power imparted, for then you can get a quick-fix, fall and rise radically changed. And you can have it all now! Behind this lies the assumption that heaven can be had on earth now, rather than having a foretaste of it.

I wondered why this experience escalated at such an alarming rate, and I believe there are several reasons; the instant factor mentioned above being the foremost. Then there is the endless quest for something new; a new direction or a new vision and change seems necessary because well worn ways are not working or bringing any results. Some pastors are weary of failure or have run out of steam and so seize something new that will hopefully avert anticipated opposition. There is the overvaluation of the capacity of imagination, for instance in 'pictures.' Then there is the fact that we attach such importance to charismatic personalities which is dangerous, because we are all too ready to accept their utterances. The desire for the sensational and spectacular to alleviate boredom and monotony is another reason. Above all, there is a lack of balance between the written Word of God and the Person of the Holy Spirit.

What I find so very sad is the undervaluing of the old

well-proved qualities of patience, endurance and faithful-ness, so that these are no longer highly esteemed. There is an insistence on receiving all the benefits of the Gospel, without the corresponding willingness to pay the price in sacrifice and suffering. I believe this is due to a lack of preaching on the Cross and on the Blood. There is a lack of repentance, humility and tears. And last, but by no means least, is the lack of knowledge of the Word of God, due to the over-valuing of singing and an under-valuing of preaching. Few even have quiet times these days. We have thus lost our Scriptural authority. In some charis-matic circles the final authority rather than being the Word, has become the Spirit, which is very subjective. Moving gradually and imperceptibly away from divine Biblical authority, we have been, and I believe still are, in danger of losing our vital anchor. Consequently, we have become vulnerable to all types of current deceptions. We have moved to 'another gospel' and 'another spirit,' which are actually "seducing spirits and doctrines of devils." 1 Tim 4.1.

I spent many days searching through the Scriptures to get a Biblical perspective of these manifestations, and I was not disappointed. I began to understand how the Scriptures had become distorted and how suspect were the current hermeneutics.

**Laughing** – is rarely mentioned in Scripture, though there is a considerable reference made to weeping. See Eccl 7.34, Jas 4.9, Lk 6.21,25. All other laughter is associ-ated with scorn, except when the Israelites recounted their deliverance from Babylon.

**Drunkenness** – The disciples were not drunk on the

day of Pentecost, because they were able to convince three thousand people of the truth of the Gospel, and no inebriated person could do that, Also, Peter actually underlined this when he said; "These are not drunk as you suppose." Acts 2.15 and 2.41, Drunkenness is always associated with depravity in Scripture and never with the Holy Spirit.

***Animal noises*** – such as roaring were heard at godless festivals. See Jer 51 38–40. There are two personalities who roar like lions in the Bible, "God who roars from heaven." Jer 25.30 and the devil who "Walks about like a roaring lion." 1 Pet 5.8. We should not attempt to imitate God's roar of judgment for this is His prerogative alone. Surely we would not want to imitate the devils roar either! Animal noises have their counterpart in covens and satanic temples.

***Falling*** – There are two types of falling in the Bible; the falling backwards of the enemies who arrested Jesus in the garden of Gethsemane, and the falling forward of John in Revelation, at the feet of Jesus and in awe of His majesty. In both instances the people involved were fully conscious and yet each case was vastly different. I believe that on the Day of Judgment we can expect that Jesus' enemies will be propelled backwards at the sight of His holiness and the conviction of their sin. Conversely, the friends of Jesus who love and obey Him will fall forward on their knees, or prostrate on their faces before Him, in total wonder and praise.

***Blowing*** – or directing the Spirit is not possible, for Jesus tells us "The wind blows wherever it pleases, you hear it but you cannot tell where it comes from or where it is going. So it is with everyone born of the Spirit." Jn

3.8. How can we, mere human beings, dare to think we can blow God's Spirit about and direct Him where to go!

Regarding these manifestations, I would like to pose a question. Do we ever read in the Scripture about any of the prophets, apostles, disciples, saints or even Jesus Himself being involved in such manifestations? The answer is no. If it was so, the New Testament would surely have something to say about it, but it does not. The manifestations of the Holy Spirit talked about in 1 Cor 12 and 14 are; tongues, healing, prophecy, words of knowledge, wisdom, miracles, faith, discernment of spirits and interpretation of tongues. These are the signs and wonders Luke tells us about in the Acts of the Apostles. Other types of manifestations occur at the close of the age, as Joel prophesied and Peter reaffirmed in Acts 2.19, 20. "I will show wonders in the heaven above and signs on the earth beneath, flood and fire and vapour of smoke. The sun will be turned to darkness and the moon to blood, before the great and notable Day of the Lord come."

Problems arising from this phenomenon are manifold: There has been a diminished emphasis and a deficient diet of the Word of God, which eventually leads to famine. I believe we are in a famine now. I can find only a few people in Bible believing churches who read their Bibles daily. There is a distraction of our attention away from Jesus, the Cross and from voluntary suffering for Him which leads to glory. There are distortions of the Scripture and short-cuts to holiness due to unrealistic expectations. There is a wrong focus on the Spirit instead of Jesus. Disillusionment arises when there is an evaporation of the so-called 'blessing.' Surely there is suspense of the mind in some, when we are clearly called to "*Test* all things." 1 Thes 5.21. Deception is on the increase and always the danger of further false 'moves' being accepted as genuine works of God. An 'experienced-centred living' can so easily replace a 'walk of faith.' There is the deadening of the senses through deafening music and worst of all, the unsaved sees the Christian as crazy and self-centred in a world that is in turmoil and desperate need. They know that this is not how the church should be behaving.

It must be obvious to you now that my view is this experience is not a move of God. Although it may appear to temporarily benefit some, it is not permanently satisfying. I feel sad and burdened that so many gracious and godly Christians have been deceived by this. They are convinced that the source of their 'blessing' is the Holy Spirit, and would be horrified to learn that it could well be simply a psychological phenomenon, or worse still a demonic influence. The call goes out "You foolish Galatians, (Christians) who has bewitched you?" Having the time to study the Scriptures on this matter and then seeing plainly what they teach, I just long for a return to biblical roots, with the Word of God as our prime source and authority, so that we are kept from errors that are stalking the church. I pray, as many others have, that there will be a return to sanity. Surely something macabre is going on when obviously crazy manifestations are regarded by eminent Christians as acceptable, even desirable and indeed of the Holy Spirit. We need to be rescued from such delusions and saved from future ones.

## Caught in a cult

*If by my death t'would bring her back to you, I'd die,*
*I would be glad to Your most holy will comply.*
*In childhood all for her I gave; Lord hear my sigh.*
*For my dear child, my only child, I weep and cry.*

*In adulthood I let her go. I did not pry*
*Into her secrets, or her lifestyle – just stood by,*
*To be there, just for her, but vainly did I try?*
*For my dear child, my only child, I weep and cry.*

*Lured by another gospel, trapped, not knowing why,*
*Drawn by this dark world's goals, she bravely once fought shy.*
*From hardened, loveless company she used to fly.*
*For my dear child, my only child, I weep and cry.*

*I had a treasure that no gold on earth could buy;*
*A loving, gentle child – with sin she ne'er did vie.*
*Yet death of soul, is what I see, and seeing cry.*
*For my dear child, my only child, I weep and cry.*

*With tears upon my bed, with agony, I lie.*
*With hopings, yearnings, questionings, Lord to You I ply.*
*Teach me to trust You for her, though her life's awry.*
*For my dear child, my only child, I weep and cry.*

*From hell's dark jaws and satan's claws I do defy*
*I bind myself to trust, to pray, till she comes nigh,*
*Back home, back to that wondrous saving cross on high.*
*For my dear child, my only child, I weep and cry.*

# An open home

# CHAPTER 15

"... A lover of hospitality." Titus 1.8

Having an open home was always a joy, but of course it kept me very busy. We were blessed with three beautiful, large vicarages during Tony's ministry and many people dropped in on us unexpectedly and often shared our meals. At first, having three young children kept me very much in the home. Since there was a huge playroom and garden, there was plenty of scope for a wide selection of fun activities which drew in other children from the town. Sometimes the vicarage was literally swarming with them and when precious toys were broken as they were bound to, I had to bite my tongue. Often, after being persuaded by the children, we would allow a friend or two to stay overnight and have to rustle up toothbrushes and pyjamas!

Later when the children were a little older, I had more time to be more involved with the parish. At various times in Tony's ministry we hosted the church prayer meeting and bible studies, youth fellowship and the young wives groups, depending on the needs of the church we were in. I also became involved with quite a lot of counselling, mostly in our last church. I was not a trained counsellor per se, except through the application of Scripture, my own experience and the psychology I had learned at the London Bible College. I did not advertise this ministry, but people came anyway and I felt obliged to help. When the more mature came on a regular basis, I found it particularly difficult and I did not look forward to these sessions, but rather dreaded them. Counselling the young however was quite another matter, for here I found I was in my comfort zone. Sadly, one young person obviously had serious mental heath problems, and I clearly remember the Lord warning me to answer her questions only by putting the relevant scriptures in front of her and asking her to read them aloud, which she willingly did. This was fortunate indeed, for not long after this, tragically she committed suicide and some of the church leaders blamed me. When I explained how I had counselled her, they could not hold me responsible.

When there were conferences taking place in our town, we would host the delegates, sometimes as many as six at a time and on one occasion ten crowded in. Tony and I would give them cooked breakfasts and refreshments at night when they returned. We also had overseas students in the summer. On occasion we had people to stay, usually young men, who were leading a mission in the parish, and we had missionaries or visiting speakers either for Sunday or for the weekend. Once I arrived home after church to cook a roast lunch and I felt tired and strained. I suddenly snapped and lost my temper and I knew that the visiting preacher, Mr. Pluckrose must have heard, even though I was in the kitchen and he in the sitting room with a large hall in between. I went straight to him and announced "I've just blown up and I'm sorry." His reply was this, "I go to many vicarages and I hear many rows, and when the vicar's wife sees me she smiles innocently as though *nothing* had happened. This is the first time I've heard someone owning up!"

We had many needy people, both to a meal or to stay, and sometimes for long periods. There were some with mental health problems, two drug addicts, two prostitutes and many sad, upset people who needed tender loving care. I was once asked whether there were any times when my husband and I felt it was inappropriate to have people with such great problems staying with us while we had young children. The answer was never, for we believed and proved that the Lord can and does protect those doing His work.

On one occasion, we were ourselves in need of help. (I am reminded of Jesus asking Peter if He could use his boat.) We were moving away to a new parish and unbeknown to us we received help from a petty criminal, called Duncan Bullock, who later changed his surname to Dyason. He arrived at our church and offered to assist us with the packing, which we gladly accepted. He was only about nineteen years old and had suffered a horrendous childhood. He had been thrown out of his home and all his worldly goods scattered outside the house. Then one day he called out "God, if you're there, help me." The Lord answered him, led him to our town and then to our church. I met him there on his first Sunday, sat and talked with him and then invited him back home for lunch. When we arrived at the vicarage, my back was hurting so much that I had to lie flat on the kitchen floor. I pointed Duncan to the cooker where all was prepared and asked him to cook the vegetables! After lunch, my back had recovered enough for us to have a walk, then tea and then back to church for the evening service. He was a little wary because he had rarely darkened a church door. The members of the congregation were very kind to him, a new vicar arrived, and soon Duncan came to know the Lord as Saviour. Amazingly, he then trained at a Bible College and on hearing of the Guatemalan street children, he left England with his young family and, without any backing from a missionary society, went out onto the streets to rescue lost, broken young lives. Eventually he established both a boys and a girls home. The story of all this and much more is in a book called 'Miracle Children.' It became the Christian book of the year.

At one church where Tony ministered, we had a very large youth fellowship that met in our home. Often members would turn up at any time, just to chat or to receive counsel or prayer. Many were students who came from the local university or polytechnic and were glad to be invited to a meal. One very cold winter, when the temperature was minus 10°C, we arranged for six young people to stay with us so that they could attend a one week mini discipleship training course with Youth With A Mission, fifteen miles away at Holmstead Manor. I opened the curtains and snow covered the landscape making it very beautiful on the morning we were due to start the course, but the roads were solidly impacted with ice. There was expected to be bad weather all week and I did not want to disappoint them by cancelling the course, and so I drove them there each morning, stayed with them during the day, and then drove them home again at night in the dark, literally taking all our lives in my hands. We obviously needed a good cooked breakfast and a hot evening meal, so it was quite a pressurised time, but also one that was beneficial to us all. Looking back I wonder how I managed, especially as I am not a very confident driver. The Lord protected us all in spite of my folly!

## When Snow Arrives

*What awed emotions stir when snow descends at night?*
*At once enthralled, as curtains drawn aside, we peep*
*Through frozen window pane and all around is white.*
*It's fallen silently, when most were fast asleep.*
*Tall fir trees bangled now with glistening jewellery bright*
*Showered down from heaven above; on us its treasures heap.*
*The rising sun has shed its golden beams of light*
*Enhancing this majestic scene; and hearts can leap*
*For wondrous joy that snow has cleansed the earth from blight*
*Of winters drabness; a freshness we can also reap.*
*Before our eyes such beauty brings its sheer delight,*
*Transforming darkening days, that ever grow more deep*
*Into a wealth of marvel at this glorious sight –*
*A memory within, to ponder, wonder at, and keep.*

Then there was Irene and she was my greatest treasure. Her photo holds a permanent place on our mantlepiece, alongside other special people in our lives, such as Philip, my nephew, who has Down's syndrome. Irene used to come to our church and to the vicarage. She was a middle aged woman who was a physical and mental wreck; a lost soul if ever there was one. She would turn up and unburden herself for hours and although I tried to help her, sometimes it seemed in vain. I learned to love Irene and she learned to trust me. She told me years later the reason she was able to do that was because I trusted her to look after my three children for an afternoon in her house. It amazed her and looking back it amazes me! Why on earth did I do that? Was I out of my mind? No, it was truly of the Lord!

One day Irene was walking down the Archway Road and I caught up with her and put my arm through hers. (Someone saw me do that and later told me, "Don't you know who that woman is? You shouldn't be associating with her!") We walked on a little further and then Irene told me that Jesus had been talking to her in her garden. I responded by telling her that Jesus talked to Mary Magdalene in a garden, whereupon she rounded on me and exclaimed, "How did you know?" I had never revealed to her that I had known all along that she was a prostitute and I did not answer her question. Instead I invited her home with me so we could talk to Jesus together. She came up to our bedroom and we knelt by the bed. Then and there this miserable, dejected, pitiful, broken woman poured out her heart to the Lord. She wept bitterly over her sin. She repented and asked Jesus to forgive her and she opened her heart to receive Him as her Saviour.

Steadily over the next few months I could sense small changes; small because there was a 'hold' on her life that needed breaking. A mega event occurred one day and I say this because it was so unusually dramatic. First Irene told me that she could not get free from her pimp, and then she went on to say that she loved him, which seemed strange. The story of Jesus cleansing the temple came straight into my mind, overturning the tables of the money-changers, who loved their ill gotten gains. I put my shoe on a sturdy, small, round coffee table and said sternly to Irene, "This is what Jesus thinks of your relationship with this man," and with that, I swept my shoe off the table so that it went flying, table and all! "Get rid of him," I said. "Have nothing more to do with him. Now go and do as the Lord has commanded you." With God's almighty power, she managed to extricate herself from the grip of this man. Praise His Wonderful Name!

Irene's life now really began to change; she had not only come to know Jesus as her Saviour, but also as her Lord. She became on fire with love for Him. Though previously mentally ill, and a woman who had only ever worked as a prostitute, she was so amazingly healed by the Lord that she was able to train to become an established civil servant. It was almost unbelievable! The transformation in Irene's life was a testimony to the mercy and great power of the Lord. She was so grateful to Him for rescuing her out of the mire and setting her feet on the rock of Christ, that she seized every conceivable opportunity to share Him with whoever would listen. She used to knock on doors and implore people to turn to the Saviour.

She often came to stay with us when we had moved away from London, and I can honestly say she was like salt and light in our home. If there was a TV programme on with even the slightest hint of violence, sex or drunkenness for example, she would tell us to turn it off immediately. Obviously we were not in the habit of watching such things, but sometimes a seemingly innocent programme can deteriorate very quickly. Irene's constant refrain after every sentence she uttered was; "Praise You Lord and thank You Jesus." She brought the sweet aroma of Christ wherever she went. When she had to be moved into an old people's home she was always clutching her Bible. She died a few days before her ninetieth birthday. Irene is the greatest token of God's transforming power I have ever seen and I count it a great privilege to have known this lady, who truly became a holy woman of God and one of my dearest friends. Heb 13.2, recommends that we entertain strangers, for by doing so; some of us have entertained angels without knowing!

# An attempted murder

Paul tells us, "I have been exposed to dangers often."
2 Corinthians 11.26

As I mentioned in the last chapter, we had many visitors and one was Jane, a lively, loving girl in her twenties who came to our church regularly. However, she had four children by four different fathers, the first of whom was taken for adoption when she was only a young teenager. Jane was married to Rex and had two children living at home at this stage, and she was finding life a struggle. They lived in a three roomed flat consisting of a kitchen, bathroom and a living room. One day I discovered that Jane's youngest, still a baby, was dehydrated, and so I rushed him by car to the nearest A&E department where he was immediately admitted. I remember seeing him lying in his hospital cot with an intravenous drip in his scalp. He was in a very sorry state.

At the same time, I was trying to help a drug addict called Susan, by supplying her with such essentials as food and blankets and attempting to get the Gospel across to her. She had a partner called Derek and two children. The couple were petty criminals and known to the police. To my horror I discovered that they were sponging off this very vulnerable couple and had actually moved in with them. I believe that Derek was the father of one of Jane's children and that he had put pressure on her. There were now eight people living in three rooms with very little space, a baby who had just come out of hospital and poor hygiene, not to mention the risk that co-habiting with criminals posed. I warned Jane of the possible dire consequences of allowing the situation to continue, but to no avail. I then threatened her by saying that unless she got rid of this family, she would no longer be able to come to the vicarage, which she loved doing. It was very hard for me to say this, but I was fearful for her future, and I could think of no other way of persuading her.

Jane must have told Susan and Derek of my threat, for one night at about midnight, the door bell rang. At first we did not answer it, but then we heard banging and shouting. Tony went to the window at the opposite side of the house and opened it. There below were Susan and Derek. "Can we come in?" they called up. Tony told them this was not a good time, but that they were welcome to come back in the morning. The next thing we heard was "If you don't let us in, you'll regret it." Reluctantly, Tony went down and opened the door and then mayhem broke out. Derek grabbed Tony and there was a violent tussle. Derek kicked Tony in the mouth so badly that it took six months to heal. I could hear the commotion and then the sound of someone rushing up the stairs. I was in my bedroom and so I quickly locked the door. It was Susan and she was pushing furiously at the door. I pressed on the other side of the door with all the strength I could muster, putting one foot on the wardrobe behind me for leverage, but the lock burst open and Susan entered. Derek then joined her and between the two of them my body was thrown from one piece of furniture to the next and my head used like a hammer against the walls until they finally knocked me unconscious. Apparently Derek then opened a window and tried to push Tony out onto the stone patio beneath, but thankfully Tony was the stronger of the two men. I was taken to Pembury hospital and seen by a consultant called Gordon Lavy, who later became our children's guardian when we went to Hawaii.

At that time we had taken in a girl called Linda Johnson, who had been badly treated and had just had surgery for melanoma on her leg. She was with us in the house that night and she managed to ring the police, which I am quite sure saved our lives. The screams were heard on the opposite side of the road, and yet our own children slept peacefully and were blissfully unaware of what was going on. A blind lady in our congregation had just turned the radio on and she picked up a police call on shortwave; there was something going on at the vicarage and the police had been called. Immediately she began to pray. The police arrived and took Susan and Derek away and they went to prison for four years for attempted murder.

When I returned home I was badly bruised and had lost a lot of hair which had been pulled out during the attack. I was in a deep state of shock, had temporary memory loss and developed fibromyalgia and my spinal problems were exacerbated. The church authorities were very kind and helped us. The Rural Dean offered us his Labrador as a guard dog which we did not take up, although we appreciated his generosity enormously and the Archdeacon arranged for locks to be fitted on all the windows, an extra bolt on the front door and a spy-hole. An alarm system was installed and the Bishop sent us to Mabledon to recuperate. No human counsellor was offered, for perhaps at the time this practice was less common, however the Lord was our counsellor. He is the "Wonderful Counsellor, the Mighty God, the Everlasting Father and the Prince of Peace." Is 9.6

The end of Jane's story is a sad one, which causes me great regret. A little while after the attack, she came into my kitchen and we sat down and talked. I had just seen her on TV on the local news and she had been pushing a pram and had, or so the newscaster reported, been smoking marijuana. I remember getting a word from the Lord for her which I uttered with great solemnity, "Jane, you must get right with the Lord, otherwise you will come under judgment." A week later, Jane came again and we talked whilst I did the ironing. Suddenly, I felt a quickening of the Holy Spirit and I began to shake violently. I walked round the room, and still shaking I said to Jane "You must get right with the Lord NOW. There is no time to lose!" I went on repeating this, but Jane did not repent and she went back home in the same spiritual state as she came.

One evening soon after this, the Rural Dean rang to say that "a lady called Jane is in hospital and she is calling for you." I had been out shopping all day and I was tired. I had felt a nudge from the Lord earlier that I should stop, and as it was seven o'clock in the evening and I had to put the children to bed, Tony and I both agreed that we should wait until the morning to go and see her. It was first thing the next morning, after the school run and I was putting on my coat to go and see Jane, when the phone rang. It was her husband Rex and he told me that she had died. I was utterly mortified because I had not responded to someone in such great need. Jane had been operated on for appendicitis at the same time as having pancreatitis, and this combination brought on a myocardial infarction which killed her. I can still hear her calling my name today, "Gillian, Gillian." and I was not there for her. I am sure she had wanted me to pray with her and I had missed a golden opportunity to lead a precious young woman back to the Lord Jesus. She was only twenty eight years old.

To complete the story of these five people, I must tell you, that although Linda had such a virulent form of cancer, she completely recovered and married Steve Treherne. After forty years of being out of touch, I have recently met up with her again, and it is a tremendous joy to me, and I believe to her too. Linda is a very special person in our lives and someone for whom we thank the Lord. She is a vivacious and very courageous lady.

I cannot end this chapter without returning to the fact that we were nearly murdered, however as Ps 18 declares and we have proved "The Lord is my rock, my fortress and my deliverer, in whom I can take refuge. He rescued me from my powerful enemies who were too strong for me." Praise His wonderful Name!

# A sabbatical in Hawaii

# CHAPTER 17

"He makes me to lie down in green pastures; He leads me beside the still waters, He restores my soul, He leads me in the paths of righteousness for His Name's sake." Psalm 23.2, 3.

A sabbatical is exactly what Tony and I needed after twenty four years of exacting ministry. But a sabbatical in *Hawaii* was too good to be true! Yet that is exactly what the Lord had planned and provided for us. It all began when a young Jewish lady called Ann Lipson came to stay with us and introduced us to the existence of Youth With A Mission, commonly known as YWAM. Soon after that we heard this organisation was holding a day conference at Ashburnham and so we decided to attend it. We were really impressed and soon began to discuss the possibility of going on one of their three month Discipleship Training Schools. We wondered whether this would be beneficial and in God's plan for us, and also what problems we would encounter if we went.

We discovered that a Discipleship Training School (DTS) for mature students, like ourselves, was only available in Hawaii and was called 'Cross Roads.' It was an exciting but daunting prospect. We were not sure where finance for this venture would be obtained or whether the Bishop would agree to our idea. Being an academic, his thoughts were that Tony should spend some time at Cambridge University studying. However, rather reluctantly, permission was granted and we were helped by a generous cheque from the Diocese. This combined with our usual three months salary would provide the beginnings of a possibility. We contacted YWAM, submitted our testimonies and were accepted. We arranged and paid for the flight with our local travel agency. Outstanding were the fees for the course and the cost of accommodation. It so happened that there was a recession in America at the time and the exchange rate was 2.4 dollars to the pound. Hotels were practically empty and were willing to accommodate guests at very reasonable prices. YWAM seized on this opportunity and took over the ground floor of a five star hotel called the Kona Lagoon. We were amongst the few who were assigned to this luxury.

With great excitement we flew from Heathrow on January 1st 1981 and landed at Los Angeles. From there we flew to Honolulu, almost missing the flight to the Big Island because we found ourselves in the wrong terminal! A Japanese man, seeing our plight came to our rescue and kindly drove us to the correct one. There, to our amazement was a small Cessna airplane with only eight seats, ready and about to take off. We only just made it, but I was worried that there was some kind of mistake or that something must have gone drastically wrong for there was only this flimsy plane available! Not so Tony, who sat beside the pilot and was in his element! Actually, as it turned out, this plane trip had been specially arranged by our travel agent as a surprise when he heard that we had never travelled beyond Europe as a couple! As we crossed Maui, the pilot climbed steeply over the extinct Haleakela volcano and then swooped down again. I was so terrified that we would crash into the mountain that I shut my eyes and failed to see this splendid sight. The pilot told us that he had only managed this feat four times in the ten years that he had flown between the two islands, because the wind and weather had to be perfect for safety. We were thus privileged to have had this adventure.

We arrived at the YWAM base early in the morning, feeling very hungry and had our first experience of missionary training, for no food or drink was available until lunchtime. There were eighty people on the course, ranging from thirty five to eighty years old. We were nearly fifty at the time. Many of the students came from the US, but from other countries too. We, with our Oxford accent, were reckoned to be very posh and they mimicked us relentlessly. The lectures were held in a large open building with only a roof and supporting posts. The first week was given over to the Quaker Questions, an icebreaking exercise, the purpose of which is to allow people to share some things about themselves and to build trust in the group. I had not come across this before, but I experienced the power of this in people's lives. We sat round in a large circle and were asked in turn for our name and then where we lived. More searching questions followed; the first being "What was the coldest time in your life?" And the second was "When did you first experience love?" Upon hearing these questions some people began to weep and sob uncontrollably. They poured out the grief in their lives, perhaps concealed for years and then they received ministry and prayer. Thus, as there were so many hurting people, what should have taken one week, took a fortnight.

From then onwards, the lectures began. From Monday to Friday morning different well known speakers would come and teach their particular subject. They were largely excellent and all lectures were recorded. At the end of each week we received an anonymous gift of the audio tapes and it was not until the end of the course that we discovered who had been our benefactors. They were a couple called George and Donna Loving, and what an appropriate surname! Afternoons were spent doing practical work duties to support the Mission. Tony was assigned to be the 'trash man' and I was given a variety of different jobs, all of which unfortunately exacerbated my spinal problems. It was not long, therefore, before I was allowed to be released from work duties on health grounds, and was free to return to the Kona Lagoon five miles away from the base. The only other student given permission to 'escape' was a Japanese man called Mr. Takaki. He had a car, but was used to driving on the left as we do here in Britain and he found the adjustment to driving on the right in America very difficult. In fact I felt he was the most dangerous driver I have ever *needed* to be driven by! I was so desperate to get to the comfort, quiet and restfulness of Kona Lagoon that I was willing to go with him despite the risk of having an accident.

The purpose of our sabbatical was, after all, not only to

learn, but to rest and get refreshment. So while all the other students had to do their own personal jobs, such as washing, cleaning and letter writing on Saturdays and weekday evenings. I was able to do ours each week day afternoon. We were also given permission to skip the Sunday morning service and just go to the important and lengthy evening service at the base. Both of these concessions gave us every evening and most of the weekends free to relax. We walked and we swam and we travelled around the island. We visited Hilo, which was a beautiful lush part of the island, whereas Kona was very barren and dry and strewn with black lava due to the volcanic activity which always continues. We would often just sit in the sun and take things easy.

## Gazing at God's creation

*Gazing at the beauty of this place,*
*Leaving pressure's hold on time and space,*
*Yielding to this rare and needed space,*
*Sensing something of God's wondrous grace,*
*Seeing now afresh my Saviour's face,*
*Falling into Jesus' warm embrace.*

*Soaring like a seagull high and free,*
*Listening to the rollers out at sea,*
*Watching as the clouds begin to flee,*
*Celebrating sunset's glorious spree,*
*Waiting as the darkness falls round me,*
*Finding I'm alone, and yet with Thee.*

*Doing nothing, still and quiet, at rest.*
*Ceasing from the work that makes me stressed,*
*Loving being on this mountain crest,*
*Knowing that for me God's got the best,*
*Riding on towards my life's great quest,*
*Being ever with you Lord; I'm blessed.*

With awe we would watch the magnificent sunsets and hope that we would see the 'green flash' as the sun disappeared below the horizon, but we never did.

## Sunsets

*What great glorious beauty permeates the skies*
*As brightest evenings turn to dusk, and sunsets*
*Glowing in the heavens high above arise*
*To feast my soul upon; resembling banquets*
*Prepared entirely new. My shrewd longing eyes*
*Are kept riveted, while yet my heart regrets*
*I've missed the start, and, might miss the end surprise.*
*But right now, I'm thrilled with coloured silhouettes*
*All weird merging streaks, changing in shape and size.*
*Sky ablaze and decked with myriad pirouettes*
*Reveals this miracle; words can't verbalise*
*The total impact. I stand like statuettes –*
*Glued to heaven's display. No one can eulogise*
*Enough to describe this drama, which now sets*
*Before us such delights. Oh what enterprise*
*Is this, that furnishes my soul and then lets*
*Me soar in wonder and freshly realise*
*How awesome is our God. Amazing assets*

*He bestows, which constantly materialize –*
*And by such famed radiance our world attests*
*This clear evidence, no human can disguise –*
*God's* transcendence *is in all that He invests.*

Finally, I enclose a poem which speaks of the stillness of those wonderful days spent in Hawaii, times when we had nothing particular to do and could pause, reflect, be quiet, be still and thus be restored.

## Stillness

*When all is still, and quiet within my soul now reigns*
*And world's pursuits are rightly seen as bitter strains,*
*Then Living water streams can flow, to fill the veins*
*Of thirsty heart and troubled spirit; all that drains*
*And robs us of the balm of peace; and then restrains*
*Our lips from joyful songs, that should be our refrains.*

*O blessed stillness, given to hearts that stop to hear*
*That sweetest voice of Him, Emmanuel, so near*
*To wounded crushed and driven souls, possessed by fear.*
*A stillness, hushing every murmur, every tear,*
*As though the world had stopped, was silent for a year –*
*But really only minutes given; precious, dear.*

*This stillness cannot be our constant soul's delight,*
*For pressures come and go in world where we must fight*
*To hold the truth, declare its glorious light.*
*But we should know His touch of stillness, in the night*
*Of cruel battles raging round us in their might.*
*And all because we know our Saviour holds us tight.*

*Sit still my child, and see His ways in you fulfill.*
*Drink in the sheer delight of being with Him – till*
*Each nerve be loosed, each sinew softened by His skill.*
*Then let your heart recapture something of the thrill*
*Of what it means to rest in His safe arms; refill*
*Your restless spirit with His peace; be still, be still.*

We visited the Mauna Kea volcano and had a reckless wish that it would erupt whilst we were there, so that we could see this amazing sight, but the volcano was soundly asleep! We visited white sandy beaches where the sand had been imported from two thousand miles away as the sand in the Big Island is normally black. I surf-bathed on the Pacific rollers which was terrific fun and happily this did not affect my back. A very kind couple called Roy and Barbara Vicory enabled us to do all this travelling by taking us everywhere in their car. What a blessing! The weather was perfect and usually about 75°F, but it was rather monotonous compared with the varied British climate. Flowers bloomed everywhere like beautiful weeds. There was Bougainvillea, Hibiscus, Jacaranda and many other varieties. The food was designed by the Galloping Gourmet, Graham Kerr, who had been on a previous DTS. It was very healthy and very plain. Our breakfast and weekend food was given to us from the base, which we had to cook in our bedroom in the hotel. Here the local 'Flea Market' came in very useful, for it provided us with a kettle and an electric frying pan at minimal cost. All the men lost weight, while all the women put it on and we were grateful for the YWAM boutique which supplied us with the right sized clothes at no cost at all. You simply chose what you needed and left behind anything you no longer required for others to use.

Strangely, I found myself becoming rather rebellious at having to attend the endless compulsory meetings on top of all the lectures. The fact that my great, great, grandfather had instituted Edward VII into Freemasonry emerged, which revealed itself in this rebelliousness. Arthur Katz ministered to me and prayed with me about the hold this had on my life. This proved invaluable to us for a future church we would lead, where Freemasonry was rife. (This is recorded in the chapter entitled 'Brushes with the law.')

There was a delightful game played throughout the entire three months we were at YWAM. It was called 'Angels and Mortals.' Everyone was an angel to one mortal and everyone was a mortal who had one special angel! Of course the angels knew who their mortals were, but not vice versa. The idea was that every angel gave little anonymous gifts or a letter of encouragement to their particular mortal. I kept receiving the most boring presents and I kept asking Tony if he had discovered the identity of my angel. I pestered him relentlessly but to no avail and of course he did not tell me, so I guessed that he did not know. Then the great Revelation Day came for the angel and mortal game. Tony was one of the last to reveal his mortal and by this time I had begun to suspect the truth, especially as he had never had the faintest clue what present to give me at home! He stood up and quoted Judges 16.16 "With much nagging, Delilah pestered Samson day after day until he was tired to death!" Then Tony announced; "Now I can tell you the truth. Gillie …

I am your angel!" The whole place erupted with laughter!

At YWAM we learned many new songs, taken directly from scripture, which brings back such happy memories when we sing them here, such as Ascribe Greatness. We also learned many valuable lessons, two of which I will recount. The first lesson was the occasion when the director of the mission gave a memorable talk and then asked for those who were willing to relinquish certain things, to stand up. First on the list was 'personal reputation' and I stood up with alacrity and so did Tony, the next was 'our home' and again I stood up first followed by Tony. We made no further relinquishments, but these two were essential for us, because later God would take us up on them. When we moved to our next parish and my father died, we lost the house that had been bequeathed to me, due to the insertion of a codicil in the will and also we most certainly lost our reputation. Both areas of relinquishment proved to be spiritually good for us and we thank the Lord for removing these idols from our lives.

The second and a most vital lesson we learned was that of 'ministering in the opposite spirit' which Jesus encourages us to do in Luke 6.27–29. Here He teaches that if someone hates us, then we must love them, and if someone curses us, we must bless them. In fact we are challenged to respond in exactly the opposite way to the person who wronged us. This reaction does not come naturally or easily. However as both Tony and I sought to put this teaching into practice it increasingly became a habit, developing into a way of life, so that we were literally unable to return evil for evil. The wonderful bonus of this is that the Lord Himself ministers the love and compassion to us that we need, and so much so, that on each occasion we find an opportunity to bless someone. I have learned to welcome and seize every such opportunity that presents itself, so that it no longer holds any potent sting.

We left Hawaii with such happy memories. We bought a 'lei', Hawaiian clothes for us both, some special treasures to remind ourselves of our exotic sabbatical, one of which was some embroidery that Donna Loving had sewn for me which read, "You are of all women most blessed." The Lord gave us a verse of scripture. Luke 22.31, 32. "Behold, satan has desired to have you that he may sift you as wheat. But I have prayed for you, that your faith does not fail. When you are converted, strengthen the brethren." When we arrived at Heathrow airport, it was a very cold, grey day and we were not dressed suitably for the climate shock! After the easy going atmosphere that prevailed in Hawaii, the lilt of the songs, the twang of the guitar, the cascading Bougainvillea seen everywhere, the sound and smell of the surf splashing on the hot white sands, the lapping of the water on the black lava and above all the almost endless sunshine, we definitely experienced a culture shock too. We were given a week off from parish work to acclimatize ourselves, which was a very generous gesture and proved to be rather necessary.

The Lord had most certainly dealt with us during our sabbatical. As Luke 22.31, 32 had prepared us, we found that we had been sifted and changed. Now refreshed and renewed we were ready to strengthen the brethren in our own church. We had learned many things of inestimable value for the tough future ministry we were soon to be assigned. All our costs were covered so that we spent no more that we would have done had we had stayed at home. How we thank the Lord for His most gracious and lavish provision.

# Feet – will you go?

"How beautiful are the feet of those that preach the gospel of peace." Isaiah 61.1

## Will you go?

*Will you be sad on that Day of the Lord*
*When into His presence before Him you stand,*
*And there's no one you've brought, quite empty your hand*
*Will His words strike your soul like a two-edged sword?*

*Will He speak of the times when He told you to pray*
*To linger, and listen; in His presence to stay.*
*And you chose to do that which was pleasing to you.*
*Will His eyes pierce your being, intensely right through?*

*Will He tell how He asked you to give, and give more,*
*To send out the messengers, zealous, but poor,*
*But you withheld most, for it hurt you to give.*
*Will His face be so sad, that men did not live?*

*Will He show you the person He wished you to be,*
*With a life that is holy, so others might see*
*The wonderful Saviour, Christ Jesus, God's Son,*
*Will His heart be quite broken; His work you've not done?*

158

*O come to the place where you're willing to do,*
*To pray, and to give, and to go, and be true*
*To the calling He purposed before you began,*
*To rescue the lost, for that is His plan.*

"Mrs. March will you please sit up and put your feet on the ground," requested my doctor when he came to visit me while I was in bed with severe bronchitis. I complied, and he exclaimed "I've never seen such beautiful feet belonging to anyone of your age before!" I was surprised because I had not noticed that my feet were particularly special. Thinking back, my mother had taken great care of my feet as hers had caused her such problems. I had regular checks to make sure I had not outgrown my shoes, and I was always given the very best, which in those days was 'Start-rite."

At our last parish in which my husband ministered for fifteen years, I was pondering whether or not I should go out and do street evangelism. If I did go, how I would need these good feet! I prayed about this possibility. At the time there was a conference in the Brighton Centre, which I not only attended daily for a week, but during which I also hosted six delegates at the vicarage, transporting them and providing meals. On top of this, I was doing my usual jobs in the church. I suffered with palpitations for a few weeks afterwards and therefore my vision to go out onto the streets was put on the back boiler. Suddenly one night, I had a massive pain in my chest. I could barely breathe and dared not move. Neither could I speak to inform Tony that I felt something terrible was happening. When morning broke, I managed to whisper "Ambulance" and one was called for. The paramedics put me on a heart monitor, pronounced I had had a heart attack and took me off to the local hospital.

At this point in my life I had accepted the view, which I no longer hold, that if we have enough faith the Lord will always heal. So I told the doctors this and asked to be allowed to go home, to which they reluctantly agreed. For nearly a week I lay in bed more or less fighting for my life, or so it seemed. Then on the sixth night the Lord spoke clearly to me and said, "Choose life or death" Deut 30, 19. I was feeling so ill that I wanted to say "I choose death," but instead I managed, "Lord, I choose life." Then He said to me "I am sending you out onto the streets of this town to preach My gospel." The next morning I awoke, got out of bed, made some soup and then did some gardening! New energy and strength had surged into my body. Despite my foolhardy behaviour in resisting medical intervention for such a serious illness, the Lord in His mercy healed me regardless, and I have had no further heart problems until very recently.

It was only after the Lord's 'commissioning' that I began to think and pray earnestly about how I might actually go out onto the streets and attract enough attention for anyone to listen to the Gospel. At about this time I met an evangelist who urged me to go with him to Hyde Park Corner to get some experience that would encourage me to start this ministry. On the Sunday afternoon we went, there were many others there on their 'soap boxes' and next to ours was Lord Soper's who was an old friend of my grandfather. The evangelist spoke with great ease and having delivered his message, he more or less commanded

*Gillian's parents, John and Grace Marcon*

*Gillian as a young girl*

*Brother Dick*

*Sister Susan*

*Gillian and Tony's wedding*

*Gillian's daughters, Rachel and Sarah on Rachel's wedding day*

*Gillian's son Andrew won the chorister of Great Britain competition in 1977*

*Andrew at Lectern to play the violin during*
*our Golden Wedding celebration*

*Gillian's husband Tony*

*Rachel's classroom drawing describing her feelings*

*Gillian preaching in the open air*

*Gillian*

*Gillian carries the Cross in a prayer march*

*Gypsy funeral*

*Gillian saying goodbye to her Cross*

me to step up and do likewise. It was a scary moment and I cannot recall what I said, but I remember being heckled and feeling distinctly embarrassed!

Eventually I managed to gather together a small team consisting of two ladies, Angela Dunkley and Marie Lewis and one man, Don Lewis who had a car. They were all willing and in fact eager, to help me proclaim the Gospel in the open air. We met one day a week at the vicarage, spending the first hour in prayer, in worship and in the Scriptures. Then we launched out into the centre of town, with no preconceived ideas of what we would do or say, just trusting that the Lord would guide us. Soon after we started open air work, I was having a quiet time when I found myself thinking about an evangelist called Arthur Blessitt who had walked the world carrying a huge cross with a wheel on the end. The idea grabbed me. If only I could have a cross like that at our open airs, then perhaps we would gain more attention? I asked the Lord about this and left it with Him.

A few weeks later a lady came up to me in church and announced, "We've heard about your street evangelism, and so my husband has made you a large wooden cross. Would you like me to bring it to church next Sunday?" You can imagine my delight and surprise when she presented me with a ten foot, forty pound wooden cross, made so beautifully and with a wheel on the end! The cross was constructed in three parts, joined with brass hinges and screws, so that it could be taken apart, reassembled and easily fit into the car. (This cross is still with me in retirement. It is far too precious and has so many wonderful memories for me to ever abandon. It was erected by the pulpit of a neighbouring village church where we held our Golden Wedding service in 2008.) Thus with three women, one man and a cross we sallied forth each Friday with some trepidation and much excitement. The other two women were far better at preaching spontaneously than me, whereas I found it easier to engage in discussion with folk in the crowd.

Sometimes only one or two would listen, and at other times there was quite a good crowd. Sometimes they listened politely, but at other times were hostile and even threatening. On one occasion we had a couple of stones thrown at us, which did not cause any injury thankfully. When speaking personally to individuals, they would sometimes open up and share their worries, hopes, fears and grief, or occasionally show a desire to know more about the Lord Jesus. If I were the speaker, I would look for some clue in the crowd. For instance, I once saw a girl plaiting her hair and interweaving coloured strands of wool. I said to her "You want to look beautiful and you do on the outside, but Jesus can make you beautiful on the inside." I then proceeded to expound on this theme, somewhat hesitatingly compared to the other team members! On another occasion a man was purposely causing a distraction to the message by playing loud, inappropriate music on an electric keyboard. At first I was annoyed that we were being interrupted, but then decided that I should go and talk to him. He stopped and listened and then, after a while I requested to play his keyboard myself and use his microphone. Surprisingly he agreed and as it was Christmas week, I played carols and then spoke briefly, that is, until I was stopped by an angry shop keeper!

I can honestly say that every time we went out preaching it was different, it was special, and in fact it was uniquely satisfying. So many wonderful and amazing things happened that it is hard to remember them all and there is not space enough to tell. However, there was a day that remains firmly imprinted on my mind; I was not preaching and so my eyes were on the look out for individuals. Suddenly I noticed a crowd of about a dozen young people, probably between the ages of fourteen and nineteen years old, who were obviously 'spaced out.' I waited to see if anyone else would go and talk to them, finding myself holding back in trepidation. Yet the Lord impressed me to go and talk to them. "But Lord, how?" I found myself pleading. "How do I engage with these young people and what on earth can I say to them?" It was then that I noticed a coloured girl among the crowd with her hair standing, or so it seemed, a foot above her head, bound with a chiffon scarf and spraying over like drooping tulips. What an opportunity! I marched up to her and said, "I'm just fascinated by your hairstyle. Do tell me how you do it?" From that moment onwards we got talking, the others joining in, until eventually we were engaged in deep conversation.

These kids were on drugs, had a series of different sexual partners and expected that they might have AIDS. They had no work; I guessed that some had no decent home to go to and no hope. They wanted to fill the void with as many 'kicks' as possible. They made rude remarks and tittered. They uttered filth and spoke blasphemies, but I pressed on regardless. I was determined to tell them about Jesus and I asked them all sorts of questions; what drugs they were on, whether those two guys over there were 'pushers,' whether they were sleeping rough and why they had adopted this lifestyle. I learned a lot! Then ever so gently at first, I suggested to them the devastation some of their parents must be experiencing, the possible ruination of future marriage caused by sleeping around and the destruction drugs wrought on the mind and body. They asked difficult questions and somehow I found myself answering them exactly as it was, no holds barred.

These kids had probably never had an adult willing to be so open and honest with them on such important issues. They were amazed by my frankness, for instance about marriage, while I felt my heart turning over inside for them. They were really listening now and had quietened down, which gave me the opportunity I needed to tell them about Jesus. Unexpectedly, one of them asked me "You're on a trip, ain't yer." I adopted this terminology in order to relate to them by telling them that I was indeed on a 'trip.' "Yes," I said "I'm on a trip."

"What yer on then?"

"Well, I'm on the best, the biggest, the longest lasting, the most fulfilling and the most wonderful trip imaginable. In fact I'm on the ultimate trip!"

"What yer taking then?"

"Very slowly I answered "The Holy Spirit. Jesus said 'If anyone is thirsty, let him come to Me and drink.' By this He meant the Holy Spirit, for He is a person, you know."

"What! The 'oly Spiri'! Did you take in the 'oly Spiri'? Did yer swalla 'im or sumfing? D'you feel 'im inside of yer?"

"Yes." I replied.

"'Ow did 'e ge' in then?"

Now this was my chance to explain the Gospel. I told them that I had invited Him, the Lord Jesus, into my heart that He had been standing outside the door of my life, knocking and asking to come in. I told them how I had heard Him and opened the door of my heart and asked Him to come in, and that it had happened about forty years ago when I was about their age.

I opened up my small leather Bible and read Revelation 3.20 "Behold I stand at the door and knock. If any man hears My voice and opens the door, I will come in and dine with him and he with Me." Rev 3.20. I began to explain this scripture; *Behold* – means, take urgent notice, so shut up all of you and listen very carefully. *I stand* – means, Jesus is standing outside your life. *And knock"* – I clenched my fist and tapped the nearest fellow on the chest. "*If anyone* – You're a man aren't you," I said, "So that's you, isn't it? *Hears my voice* – You can hear me, can't you, and through me, Jesus is speaking to you. *And opens the door* – that is, agrees or chooses to let Jesus come in. *I will* – not I might, or if you pack up your drugs. No, no. If you open up to Me, Jesus says, 'I will.' It's a promise. I know everyone breaks promises but Jesus has never, nor will He ever break any promise. *Come in* – Yes, He will come into your life, He will dine with you and he will stay with you; He will take away your fears, He will heal your hurts, He will forgive your sins, He will give you hope now and security for the future. He will truly make you happy. He has done all this for me and He wants to do it for you. He paid the cost to rescue you when He died on the cross. Your sin deserves God's anger, judgement and hell and yet all He asks is that you surrender your whole life to Jesus, and let Him be your boss, for He not only wants to be your Saviour, but your Lord and Master too." It was now time to leave and so I gave them each a leaflet about salvation, said goodbye, and wended my way back to the team who had been waiting for me. The day had come to an end and we were as usual tired out and had aching feet from trudging the streets. But we had gladdened hearts that the Gospel message had gone out once more to desperately needy people. As was our custom, we went back to the vicarage for tea and cakes and of course that all important time of prayer.

Years later, I was again ill in bed, but this time in hospital. I had a severe spinal infection causing stenosis, or narrowing of the spinal cord. There was no room in any ward, so I was put in a day room, all by myself. This was hugely beneficial as regards being allowed visitors at any time, though a disadvantage in that I was not able to communicate the Gospel with other patients. Every morning, without fail, the ward sister came with a bowl of warm water, pushed back the bedding at the end of my bed and proceeded to wash my feet – only my feet. I never enquired as to why she performed this menial task for me, but I do remember her off-loading her problems, giving me a chance to share Jesus with her. It was not until later that the significance of the feet washing became apparent; this loving, gracious gesture of the ward sister brought back to mind Isaiah's words; "How beautiful are the feet of those that preach the Gospel of peace." It was as though the Lord, through this woman was washing my feet in recognition of my street evangelism but also as a sign that He was retiring me from this ministry, for never again did I have this opportunity due to increasingly poor health. I look back with wonder and gratitude, for every minute out there preaching and sharing the glorious good news of our wonderful Saviour, and I feel so blessed that He allowed me this priceless privilege.

## Those Feet – Mary Magdalene washes Jesus Feet

*What love is this that stoops so low*
*To wash His feet with tears that flow,*
*And dry them with her locks of hairs,*
*For burial soon she now prepares.*

*What love is this that pours the oil*
*So precious, yet draws such recoil.*
*A fragrance sweet that fills this place*
*And brings deep joy to Jesus' face.*

*What love is this that sees those feet*
*So beautiful; and kisses sweet*
*And tenderly; of all concerns*
*To show to Him a love that burns?*

*What love is this that knows those feet*
*Which meet great need; destroys defeat*
*With news so good for one so bad,*
*And turns to joy a heart once sad.*

*For feet that came from heav'n to share*
*The truth, and in His feet to bear*
*The curse of God for sinful man,*
*Reveal His Father's saving plan.*

For feet like this that tramped the soil
With bruised tired limbs, unceasing toil,
For love that sacrificed His all,
For feet that brought the gospel call.

For feet that walked this earth of pain
And took upon them sinner's stain,
Those purest feet that never sinned,
Yet to those feet God's wrath was pinned.

For feet that travelled many a mile
To show the sick and lost and vile
The one true message that could bring
Salvation, if to Him they cling.

For feet that climbed the mountain bare,
Alone to speak all night in prayer
And wait to hear His Father's voice,
Submit His will; agree His choice.

For feet like this that hung on tree
Of agony for you and me.
With feet pressed down and cruelly nailed
With massive blows, while voices railed.

What love will you bestow on Him,
What ardent heart, filled to the brim
With thankfulness; that feet so blessed
Have brought to you this glorious rest.

*Will you surrender now your feet*
*And be prepared to walk the street,*
*To tell of how His feet have brought*
*The life of joy and peace you sought.*

*Will you bow down and kneel before*
*Those feet of Jesus; and adore*
*The Saviour, in humility*
*And love Him for eternity?*

# The darkness of prison

# CHAPTER 19

"He has sent me to proclaim liberty to the captives and the opening of the prison to those in bonds." Isaiah 61.1

I then became a prison visitor at Lewes Prison, (although in my case more of a prison counsellor) where all were men and most on remand. As this is a Home Office appointment, credentials are thoroughly scrutinized before successful applicants are given their 'green card' which permits entry. I have to say that I found that place to be the darkest, saddest and most miserable I have ever been in, and it was with reluctance that I continued there for as long as I did.

Prison visitors can either sit and wait for their particular prisoner with the solicitors in an unlocked room, or mingle with the friends and relatives of the prisoners in a locked room. I preferred the latter, although I can quite honestly say that many of them should probably have been inside themselves, or certainly would be one day. There was one poor woman though, whose son, or so I believe, had been wrongly accused. When visiting time was called, we were all led to long wide tables, with prisoners sitting on one side and visitors on the other. For some unknown reason, best known to the Lord, I was allowed a separate room which sometimes had clear glass walls but at other times not. I was allotted sex offenders, drug dealers, two murderers and others whose alleged crimes I did not discover, probably because I did not ask. My task was not to cause them to dwell on the past, but to show them the possibility of a brighter future.

On one occasion and with some trepidation, I took my huge cross into the locked waiting room. As usual I got into conversation, but I was horrified by the filth they uttered, and yet I was to encounter *much* worse. Eventually the gross darkness of that place and in those people so gripped me that I stood up with my cross, and hesitantly began to preach the Gospel. I like to preach with notes that have been finely honed, but I did not have the luxury of such preparation time, for these folk were so needy, so utterly lost; you could see it in their troubled faces and hear it in their foul speech, that I had to speak right then! They actually listened pretty well for a while until I was stopped by a man who called me over. He was sobbing and he told me that he was a back-sliding Christian. I told him to repent and start afresh with Jesus as his Lord. I then prayed with him. Just at that moment, the door was unlocked and a guard called, "Mrs. March, will you come here." I wondered what I had done wrong. I was not aware that the guards could see everything that was going on in the waiting room via hidden cameras. He then proceeded to frisk me, and out of my anorak hood he produced a condom, which had obviously been placed there by one of the men. It was a vile act of personal violation and showed the level of their depravity.

Another time, the prison governor called me into his office and said, "Mrs. March, why are you so unafraid?" I asked him what I should be afraid of, and he replied "I carry a gun with me, I lead an Alsatian dog around with me, and yet still the hair on my back stands on end when I meet some of the prisoners."

"Well," I said, "I used to fear a lot of things, but when I came to know Jesus as my Saviour, I brought those fears to Him." And then I quoted a verse from Ps 34.4 "I sought the Lord and He heard me, and delivered me from all my fears." As I left his office he kept repeating, "Be careful, be very careful!" On one occasion I was given a black prisoner who was dying of cancer, and expected to die in jail quite soon. I am so glad I was picked for this man as I was able to pray with him and believe for him that the Lord God Almighty who has 'all the keys of the kingdom,' could let him out before he died so that he could rejoin his family in Africa. I was delighted on my next visit to find him gone. He had been released the very next day!

I was allotted one particular murderer who confessed to me that he was guilty. I saw him quite a few times. He was an old retired army officer who had come up through the non commissioned ranks to become a major and had been living in an old people's home. There he became friendly with one of the ladies, but the friendship soon turned sour and she became the source of extreme aggravation to him. One day, in a moment of unpremeditated frustration, he suddenly took a glass bottle and hit her over the head and killed her. He was awaiting sentence and all I could do was listen to him and pray with him. Each time I visited this man I prayed for his release, and praise God he was, and only placed on probation for two years.

Out of the blue, the prison governor rang me up one day and told me, "We have an African man here who can only speak his native language and French. We can't find anyone who can communicate with him in French." I mentioned that I had taken 'O'Level French three times before gaining the right grade for university! He then explained that this man was on hunger strike and would die if something was not done soon. Of course I agreed to go immediately and was with him for about an hour. During that time I spoke nothing but French, which I had not spoken for forty years! It was probably more pigeon than pukka French, but the main thing was that he understood. Then I prayed with him, "Mon Dieu, aidez cet homme s'il vous plait," I began and continued falteringly. Time was up and I had to leave. Then I did something no one is allowed to do with prisoners, I gave him something; a bar of chocolate. Three days later a familiar voice was on the phone, it was the prison governor again and I trembled. I knew my green card could, and probably would, be stripped from me, for I had broken a cardinal rule. "Mrs. March," said the governor, "since you gave that prisoner the bar of chocolate, he has not stopped eating. Thank you so very much indeed!"

Earlier on I had befriended four young lads aged around ten years old or so. They often came to the vicarage and I would tell them about Jesus. As a consequence they more or less knew what was in our house. Then one of the boys, called Martin, who had by now grown up into a teenager, was in Lewes Prison which saddened me greatly. One day we received a note through the door while we were out, informing us that the police were coming to see us. Three policemen duly arrived and told us that they had got wind of a planned robbery about to take place in our house. There was some silver displayed, a large oil painting and some Sheraton chairs and there was a plot to steal these. As it happened, the silver was plate, the oil painting a present from one of our daughters who had touched it up to look like an oil, and the Sheraton chairs were only a good reproduction! The police carrying guns, carried out surveillance on the house for two days, but nothing ever happened. This made me realise that there was a degree of danger associated in dealing with these sorts of people in one's own home, and more especially how the Lord was protecting us through this excellent policing.

The last case I was involved with was a man detained for sexual offences and I believe he was a homosexual. As was my custom with all prisoners, I hugged him on arrival. We sat and talked and he told me that he had tried to take his life the night before. He then pulled up his sleeve and showed me a large ugly cut down his arm which he proceeded to try and open up in front of me. Without a moments hesitation I reached over to try and stop him, forgetting I had an open wound on that outstretched hand. I very quickly excused myself, feeling like Lady Macbeth when she cried "Out vile spot," for the possibility of having exposed myself to AIDS stared me in the face. I went straight to the guard and asked him for water to wash myself, but none was available. I was then escorted to the prison chaplain, counselled and of course washed. Soon afterwards a letter was sent out to all prison visitors stating that prisoners must never be touched. I knew I was the culprit and I also knew that I could not abide by this rule. I felt, and still do very strongly, that touch is a most important part of ministry for the prisoners, who like all of us, need affection. Most may well be inside because they have never really experienced this.

Prison is indeed a very hard, lonely and frightening place, but I thank the Lord that I had the privilege of seeing this at first hand and gaining fresh insight into what prison really means for these poor men. I prayed that the Holy Spirit would fill me and enable me to help them. I prayed for His special anointing as I sought to proclaim God's deliverance and His Salvation to these broken lives. I know that our Mighty God is able to set the captives free and open prison doors, both literally, but more especially spiritually. Only in heaven, however, will I know if any I ministered to, received Jesus as their Lord and Saviour.

## Darkness

*What darkness looms, so few to challenge, dare.*
*Cold, lifeless, hardened, alienated hearts,*
*So seared in sin,*
*Yes deep within.*
*No thought about their destiny; no care*
*For ruined life by satans' subtle darts.*
*Lord, melt those hearts with love, these lost ones win.*

*By worldly futile pleasures lured astray.*
*Bewitched by many a rival not of You.*
*Sad empty souls,*

With useless goals.
'Tis not Your high and holy path their way,
Yet pierced with many sorrows through and through.
Lord, help us reach them ere their death knell tolls.

While darkness brood's o'er lands, shine Your great light.
Eyes blinded, open now, that they may see.
Please open doors,
And let them pause
To comprehend the graveness of their plight,
And from their self made prisons set them free.
O Lord, may these for whom we pray, be Yours.

Help us in this gross darkness brightly shine.
Clouds gather stealthily, unseen by most.
Around us all,
Our numbers small.
May we Your Word obey, our wills incline
With hearts on Jesus fixed, in Him to boast.
O Lord, in our great need, to You we call.

# The horrors of witchcraft

"Clothe yourselves ... with tenderness, pity, mercy, gentleness, patience ... and above all love." Colossians 3.12–14

Hannah, once a High Priestess of a satanist temple, arrived in our home in February 1990. She stayed with us for a month in order to give the couple with whom she had been living a rest. Mary and her husband had been pouring out their lives for her for a long time and they needed a complete break. It was also in the Lord's plan that we should learn more about a part of this depraved world of which we hitherto knew absolutely nothing, and so it was mutually beneficial. The month that we had Hannah with us proved to be a very testing time indeed; not only were we up against the kingdom of darkness in a new way, but we, or rather I, was involved with Hannah both day and night. She needed continuous care, prayer and ministry, so that sleep was at a premium. What Hannah needed was the kind of tenderness, patience, gentleness, mercy, pity and love that we read about in Colossians chapter three, and *lots* of encouragement.

Hannah was filled with fears that the satanists would drag her back to the indescribably horrific life into which they had forced her. We had a very large vicarage with high ceilings and tall windows which we were unable to curtain completely, and Hannah insisted that every window be shielded from prying eyes. I therefore had no alternative but to improvise with old bedspreads and sheets, sewing them together and draping them over any exposed sections. Hannah was a beautiful girl aged about twenty three, whom I quickly grew to love. The kind of compassion that Hannah required was of an altogether different order than I was used to giving. What was needed was the heart of Jesus; something more, something deeper and self sacrificing.

## Lord Jesus, give me your heart

*Your heart is what I need Lord Jesus, what I pray.*
*Your heart where all my burdens, sorrows I may lay.*
*Your heart from which I'm all too often prone to stray.*
*Your heart to lead my own, through life's uncertain way.*
*Your heart controlling mine; Your countenance display.*
*Your heart within my heart to ever shine and stay.*

*Give me a tender heart that for Your presence yearns.*
*Give me a prayerful heart that to You often turns.*
*Give me a humble heart that always quickly learns.*
*Give me a single heart, Your holy will discerns.*
*Give me a steadfast heart, Your bidding never spurns.*
*Give me a loving heart that for You always burns.*

My role was to love Hannah, and accept her which I did not find difficult, because I understood the devastation of rejection. I therefore never challenged her or condemned her, but I did urge her to further repentance and to receive more deliverance. I simply listened to the story of her life and shared her grief. I told her she was precious and lovely. I took her hands in mine and proclaimed her white in the blood of Jesus. I sat many hours with her, hours well spent, and a time when I learned so much that the Lord needed to teach me in order to help this tormented soul. This is the story of her life, told to me by Hannah personally, and which I am glad I wrote down and kept.

"I had a Gypsy mother, a poor father and one brother. My parents could not cope and so they put me into a home. In fact I went to many. School was a nightmare and I learned practically nothing. Being hurt and miserable, I took drugs, and to pay for these I took to the streets and was a prostitute. This led me into pornography and blackmail. I was caught by a witchcraft coven against my will, but I was so clever at the 'craft' that I became the head witch. Early on I learned to astral project.. From there I was drawn into a satanist temple. Here again, after some time, I rose to become the High Priestess, but only after excruciating experiences – either I obeyed or I was tortured. I never wanted to sacrifice anyone, but I was made to, or else … I was put in a cage for months and only let out sometimes. I was beaten and I have marks to prove it. I had to sacrifice animals and eat them raw. Sodomy was practiced on me, using a cross and in unspeakable ways. I was also put on a cross and raped.

I was made to commit murders and I was forced into cannibalism, but no trace of this is ever discovered. Bodies are melted into wax and used as candles and bones are used as jewellery. I have Danny's bones (a boy she loved and was forced to murder) as jewellery in a bank, but do not tell anyone. The covens and temple practices are a close network throughout society and indeed throughout the world. They are highly secretive, all traces of evidence being removed. Covens and temples move continually to avoid detection. Every section of the community is infiltrated. To divulge or renege is to invite dire consequences; for instance being skinned alive, crucified and then cut up into pieces. I infiltrated churches, especially the keen ones where the Holy Spirit was moving. All satanists do this. I have pretended conversion to Christ, but there came a time when I entered a Holy Spirit healing centre, and before long I was prostrate on the floor with guilt and grief; the power of God was so great. I gave my life to Christ and received Him as my Saviour. I found it very difficult to be accepted by Christians and to live the Christian life. I had, and still have many demons in me. When they manifest, they tear and batter my body and mind. I need deliverance, but I am so afraid."

Hannah wanted to live with us for ever; for us to become her adopted parents, but this was impossible in a parish situation. For the entire time Hannah was with us I had had to put a hold on all my work within the church and outside it in order to help her. Because of this, I realised she could not stay indefinitely, though part of me longed that this could have been possible. Hannah left us to go to another vicarage in Blackburn. The first day there, she wrote me a lovely card which I will include here. 'Dearest Tony and Gill, here is just a little note to say thank you so much for having me to stay with you. You have both been very good to me and I shall cherish the memories in my heart ... I am looking forward to seeing you again soon. I hope you like my poems. Remember I wasn't educated ... Please send my love to Angela and ask her please, please to write to me. Loads of love and hugs. Hannah. Xxxx.' You can imagine our grief when, the next day, the vicar in Blackburn rang to say that Hannah had taken a drug overdose and was critically ill in intensive care in hospital. My friend Claire Holden very kindly drove me all the way up to Blackburn to see her and pray with her. We waited and we prayed for twenty four hours and then we heard the sad news that Hannah had died. It was absolutely heart breaking. I wrote to the vicar and put this, "Hannah has died, but she is now with the Lord. Can you bear to hear her life story that she told me personally?" ... and that is what I did.

Soon Hannah, who had given herself this Christian name when she came to know Jesus, her real name being Caroline Marchant, was headline news in all the tabloids. In the Sunday Mirror on March 25th 1990 the headlines filled the entire front page in capital letters and read "I sacrificed my babies to satan," "From sex orgy to death at the hands of devil's disciples," "Three police forces are now investigating Hannah's confessions," and "The NSPCC said that her story confirmed their worst fears about child sacrifice and ritual abuse by satanist cults in Britain." We left Blackburn with saddened hearts, not just for Hannah, but for all those other precious lives lost to satan's schemes. Lost, frightened and tortured souls in this world, and lost in the next world too, unless they turn to the Lord Jesus Christ as Hannah had done.

# Dancing with Gypsies

"Not many wise ... not many mighty ... not many noble are called ... but the things that are despised, has God chosen." 1 Corinthians 1.26, 27

We have all heard of Gypsies, but how many of us have come to know some personally? This chapter heading expresses the sheer delight and joy of having had such a privilege. King David danced before the Lord and that is what I did with the Gypsies, not literally of course but spiritually, for I was able to draw sufficiently close to them to catch their infectious warmth and to be inspired by their zeal and fire for the Lord. How our ill conceived notions sometimes need radically changing! This was true for me regarding Gypsies. I had always thought of them as rather mysterious folk, dirty, dishonest, spongers on the community, definitely into some kind of witchcraft and their caravan camps unsightly blots on the landscape. Although there are some who fall into this category, there are a growing number of Gypsies who have come to know and love the Lord Jesus. They are in fact the largest ethnic group of Christians per capita in the world; fifty per cent now being Christians. I have found these to differ vastly from my previous image of them.

The first time I ever heard the word 'Gypsy' was when I was nine and was asked to conduct the song, 'The Raggle Taggle Gypsies!' The second was through my Aunt Muriel, (My mother Grace's sister who we nicknamed 'Aunty Penguin' because of her black and white nun's habit.) She told me she had been converted to Christianity as a young Christian through the well known evangelist Gypsy Smith while attending one of his open air meetings in London The third occasion was when I had to 'cover' a gypsy funeral for a profile I was compiling for my lay readership. It was the most magnificent funeral I have ever attended for its pomp and pageantry, with horse drawn carriage and myriads of flowers. A photo of this splendid occasion is included in this book.

The one negative characteristic most Gypsies seem to have in common is their propensity to be suspicious of outsiders. This is understandable considering the way they have been treated over the centuries; they have been marginalized, scandalized and persecuted. The Nazis killed them in their thousands in their infamous concentration camps. Most of us here in Britain avoid them or positively dislike them. Their mechanism of defence is to be suspicious and who can blame them! However, once the barriers of suspicion have been broken by vetting to ascertain the outsiders credentials as a Christian, the welcome is wonderfully warm and the Gypsies are able to let down their guard. It was not until Tony and I retired that I was invited by my friend Penny Foster to attend a Christian Gypsy meeting which met every Monday evening in Marden, a village nearby. Here she had been accepted and I went on her recommendation and was immediately greeted with open arms. In this place I discovered the joy of their worship and the love of their fellowship.

Their meetings were completely different from any I had experienced before. The men and women sat on opposite sides and all the women covered their heads with scarves. One felt an instantaneous kind of 'buzz,' a sense of expectation and excitement and I was not disappointed. Although there are talented musicians amongst the Gypsies, this did not seem to be the case here except for a lady called Sarah Ridley who struck up on her guitar and then everyone started singing with great gusto. It was incredibly enthusiastic but also dreadfully out of tune! When the prayer time came the whole gathering raised their voices in unison, so that a great swell must have reached heaven, for its fervency and integrity. Individuals also prayed spontaneously. Testimonies were encouraged which were often riveting.

Only the men ever preached and none were well educated, so the messages were quite simple, but profound and always pointing to Jesus. Often the theme was 'holiness,' 'The fear of the Lord' or 'the blood.' Particular importance was laid on the Second Coming; they sensed that the time was near, and that they were being 'gathered in.' These messages could in no sense be described as erudite, but they were powerful, challenging and indeed of the Holy Spirit. Christian Gypsies believe God. They believe the Word of God. They believe for and expect miracles, as promised in the Word, and so they receive them. If one member is sick or backslidden, great heart felt cries would be wrung from their lips, with appropriate

'Amen's' being added by all, and very often the Lord would heal and recover His erring ones. The joy of their meetings, the richness of their worship, the power of their prayers, the love in their fellowship and the 'every member participation,' struck me from the start. I did not feel strange to be amongst them at all. I got to know many of their names, hear about their children, and share their joys, concerns and aspirations. I really felt one *with* them and one *of* them and I believe I was accepted as such – an 'honorary' Gypsy!

When the European Union was formed in 1958, many Eastern Europeans swarmed into Britain. Amongst these were Gypsies who were considered to be illegal immigrants and they were eventually sent back to their country of origin. Before leaving, British Gypsy evangelists felt the call to go and minister the way of salvation to those awaiting deportation and many were transformed and returned to Europe as Christians. The Lord brought them here to Britain to reveal the Gospel to them so that they might return home to reach their own people with that same Gospel!

Some years ago I went to a Gypsy convention with Penny for a few days. It was held in Hawkesbury, near Coventry, by the Life and Light Mission. A very large field was lent to them by some kind farmer for this purpose. A huge circus tent was erected to hold the thousands of Gypsies who would attend. To find this site we had to follow special chalk signs on the ground; a form of secret communication to avoid detection by the locals who would all too readily put a stop to such an event. The police had to be involved, but when they observed the way the Gypsies conducted themselves and how immaculately they kept the site, they were so impressed that it totally transformed their previous conceptions of Gypsies. I too had my eyes opened, first by the sheer number of Gypsies with their caravans, and then by their incredibly 'posh' attire; no glad rags here, or tatty jeans, but silks and furs, as if they were going to visit royalty, which of course they were – the King of Kings! The meetings were packed, the speakers were excellent and there was no distraction from unruly children. Christian Gypsies have a high and strict moral code and prefer not to send their children to school for fear of their exposure to worldliness such as drugs, drink, foul language and promiscuity. This morality is drawn from their teaching and knowledge of the Word of God in which they place their complete trust.

We visited several Gypsies in their caravans which they call 'Vados.' These were immaculately clean and tidy and filled with such beautiful items such as Royal Dalton china and gorgeous drapes. On such visits, although we were strangers to some, we were treated with respect and generous hospitality. They shared their joys and grief with us and asked us to pray with them. Because they are often not very well educated and many are illiterate, the Gypsies *have* to learn to read and write when they become Christians in order to 'get to grips' with the Bible. They often find this difficult and yet they persevere. Some older folk never succeed and have to rely on Bible recordings.

I am no longer able to fellowship at the Gypsy Church because it has moved too far away. However Sarah, the guitarist, heard the Lord tell her to come and visit me, as I had once asked her. In twenty eight years of living here, not one Gorgio (non Gypsy) had invited her into their home. On her first visit she asked me if I would help her get the CDs she had made of her Gospel singing out to a wider public, not knowing I was musical. When I heard the recordings I was amazed at her sheer raw potential talent. She has been coming once a week ever since, and we have grown to love each other, so much so, that last time she said ' At last I have found you', and I felt just the same. Our close bond is in the Lord Jesus.

One day Sarah told me of the relentless accusations of malpractice being levelled against her at her place of work, with a view to getting her out of her job. Each time she was compelled to respond with patience and humility. Then the enemy set a trap which she almost fell into, but happily came and asked my advice in time. I said 'Sarah, so far the Lord has protected your job, so resist this snare and keep on ministering in the opposite spirit, and the Lord will continue His protection'. I gave her several Scriptures, including, "You shall not need to fight in this battle", and "Stand still and see the salvation of the Lord." She readily agreed, we prayed and Sarah went home with peace and thankfulness. Next week the health and safety inspector surprisingly arrived. The CCTV cameras were studied, everyone's work was scrutinized, and the only persons work that could not be faulted was Sarah's. The manageress commended her and I don't think anyone will dare taunt her again, nor will her job be in jeopardy. How speedily the Lord vindicated and honoured her!

I have found the Gypsies to be a most friendly people who have a lot to teach all of us in the church of God. I do not believe we can even hold a candle to their godly devotion for they put us 'Gorgios' (non Gypsies) to shame. How glad I am to have met and grown to love this ethnic community of which I was hitherto almost totally ignorant, and to find the Lord working so powerfully amongst them.

## The Gypsies

*Most likely, unlike me, you may not know*
*Who these mysterious people really are.*
*From one place to another often go,*
*Their origin from distant lands afar.*

*They seem to us peculiar and strange,*
*With sometimes darkened skin be found,*
*And caravans to dwell, of quite a range*
*In country sites, not usually renowned!*

*These shadowy figures live amongst us all,*
*And yet we on the other side pass by.*
*Their numbers only relatively small,*
*And few there be that hearken to their cry.*

*Outcasts from all the world's society,*
*So often only given short riposte*
*And considered as impropriety,*
*Of course to be avoided at all cost.*

*Down through the centuries we persecute*
*And mete to them the worst of everything.*
*Their righteous claims to justice still refute,*
*And we such harsh abuse upon them bring.*

*But not so God; His love for them is great,*
*He draws them to Himself, and so they come.*
*These folk thus marginalized, to Him relate,*
*As once the halt, the deaf, the blind, the dumb.*

*Come, peep into their worship; hear their praise,*
*And listen carefully to their ardent prayers.*
*See how their hearts to Him they often raise,*
*Consult with Him about their many cares.*

*They trust the Word of God with confidence,*
*And so experience many miracles.*
*He is to them the God of providence,*
*Removing satan's subtle obstacles.*

*The holy life to them pre-eminent,*
*With sin expunged by Jesus precious blood.*
*The second coming seen as imminent,*
*And swift and sure, as prophesied the flood.*

*We cannot hold a candle to their zeal,*
*Or in their sorrow comprehend their joy.*
*They know their God, and He to them is real.*
*They live to ever be in His employ.*

*So, spare a minute; open up your mind*
*And see afresh what God has done for them,*
*How He has been so wonderfully kind.*
*They are to Him a royal diadem.*

# Called to be an intercessor

"If My people who are called by My Name will humble themselves and pray and seek My face and turn from their wicked ways, then will I hear from heaven, and will forgive their sin and heal their land." 2 Chronicles 7.14

I believe it was from a dream I had of preaching at a university, that a ministry was born; that of intercession. I began to spend at least an hour a day in intercession alone, with further time being given to Bible study, private prayer and worship. I would like to explain what I gleaned about this most important ministry, as hopefully it will be beneficial. I am sure we *all* agree that our world is in an uncertain, worrying, chaotic and crucial state, such as we have never seen been before in its history. Outrageous acts of evil occur almost daily and there is distress and turmoil with resulting broken lives all around us. We have the spectre of wars, floods, earthquakes, famine, greed and a depletion of natural resources. Furthermore, there is terrorism, financial collapse and the risk of nuclear disaster hanging over us of epic proportions. There is also the threat of militant Islam, and the implementation of the New World Order, with a sinister dictator as described in the book of Revelation.

The question that faces us and which challenged me, is *what shall we do about it?* If the politicians can do little, then how can we? The Lord showed me, however, that we *can* and indeed *should* do something about it, for there is something more positive and more powerful than any government or army ... intercessory prayer. Even an ordinary individual like me can be involved! We may consider this ministry to be 'not quite our thing' but God has other ideas, for we are *all* called to intercession. He encouraged me to discover the value and thrill of this vital role and I have heard it said, amazing as it might sound, that interceding Christians are actually the ones holding the balance of power in this world.

The word intercession is really theological jargon for praying for something or somebody *outside* of ourselves. It is an intervention, a pleading on the behalf of another. It is a standing in the gap. It can be described as the legality of heaven being brought down to earth through prayer. The Lord showed me that the purpose of intercession is to hold back the powers of darkness created by the evil one, so that as many people as possible might hear the glorious saving Gospel of our Lord Jesus Christ; be healed in their relationships, be forgiven and restored to fellowship with a Holy God from whom they have been cut off, and thus receive His blessing. This applies to individuals, groups and nations. The purpose of intercession is to see the mighty hand of God intervene in a situation according to His perfect will.

Although I believe that God does not *need* us in order to accomplish His purposes, He has arranged for things to work by our co-operation with His plans, through prayer. If this were not true, why would He bother to ask us to "Pray without ceasing" 1 Thes 5.17 Thus I am sure that very little, or even nothing, will be achieved for the Kingdom without prayer, whether it is for our own lives, the lives of others or for the nations? Ezek 36.37 tells us "This is what the Lord God says, I *will* for this be enquired of." In other words, He wants, He even requires us to pray. I firmly believe that no one will come into the Kingdom of God without prayer, and that no one comes to the Saviour except there has been someone, somewhere, on their knees travailing in prayer. Surely neither you nor I, nor anyone else ever came to know the Lord Jesus on our own, just because we decided to. No, it was some faithful person, maybe unknown to us, gripped by God, who cared enough for us to intercede.

The reason I know that an intercessor does not have to be a special or particularly gifted person is because the Lord has chosen me! He usually uses very ordinary people and often those hidden from the spotlight. To become an intercessor does not happen just like *that* though. It is not hey presto and the gift is bestowed! It is brought about first and foremost by a 'relationship' with the Father established by trusting the Lord Jesus as Saviour and coming into a living, personal and dynamic relationship with Him. It is also established by the 'realisation' of the immensity of God's love and mercy towards us in all that He is and has done for us. Furthermore, it comes from 'recognition' of the horrendous situation of those without the Saviour, both in their present plight and in their future destiny.

I have discovered that we will face problems when we

agree to take on this ministry. The enemy of souls hates intercessors for their value to God. Thus he tries every trick to dissuade us and steal away our desire or time and therefore our effectiveness. When we resolve to intercede we begin to encounter acute attacks from satan, and if we put this ministry foremost on our agenda we will most certainly draw the powers of darkness our way. I needed to be ready, vigilant and prepared for his onslaughts. I have learned from others and through personal experience that there are many different ways in which the enemy attacks, which I will list here.

***Depression;*** a potent weapon that can hold us captive for days, weeks, months or even years if we do not allow God to deal with it. ***Distraction;*** a shower of 'other thoughts' can fill our minds and take us right off course. We might sit or kneel and think we are praying when in reality we are merely day dreaming and so the time is disturbed and unproductive. ***Delay;*** is a common problem – "I've not got the time now, but I will pray about it some other time, for after all the Lord understands." Does He, I wonder, or is it that we do not understand Him? He is looking, watching, waiting and longing for us to keep that special appointment with Him and saddened when we do not. ***Discipline lacking;*** is another way the enemy wreaks havoc. The problem of getting up earlier enough is a battle which is won the night before! ***Duty only;*** here the attitude is "Quickly pray, quickly read the Bible and quickly get it all over!" This leads to superficiality and we will be unlikely to hear God's voice. ***Disobedience;*** is another reason why we cannot 'get through' or why we do not bother. Uncleansed, wilfully pursuing our own agenda, contrary to God's promptings will leave us with no desire to meet with the living God. **Disbelief;** in the Word of God or in His ability to hear us or answer us will certainly rob us of any desire to pray.

Intercession falls into two categories; planned and unplanned. For those times that are *planned,* the main requirement is information. I need to be *informed* about what is going on in the big wide world, so I take practical steps; having a world map is helpful and I put one up on a wall where I pray. I begin to glean information from the media and circulars which highlight the various areas of need, particularly Christian ones and I use these. Then I am systematic and make a plan so that I have a frame-work for my prayers. Once informed I need to be *directed* by the Holy Spirit according to Rom 8.27. I also need *faith.* In Mark 11.24 Jesus tells us "I say to you, that whatever things you desire when you pray, believe that you receive them, and you shall have them." Furthermore I need to be expecting results. In John 16.24 Jesus says "Before you asked nothing in My name. Ask and you shall receive." Lastly, I keep a written record in order to recall answered prayers which stimulate faith for more active prayer.

For *unplanned* intercession I need to be in a place of readiness and anticipation, for these opportunities occur suddenly or unexpectedly. This is what makes it so exciting! As an intercessor I pray whenever it is possible and for any and every conceivable opportunity that might present itself, either alone or with other Christians. I aim to pray about current news items as soon as I hear about them and before I forget. I try to pray immediately when I hear of or see a person in great need. When I ask if I might pray aloud with that person I endeavour to be as tactful and winsome as possible and yet be bold. It is so easy to miss these priceless opportunities and fail to bless people by hesitation or procrastination. I believe that an intercessor is someone who does far more than just saying prayers in a brief perfunctory fashion. These will not move the hand of a holy God. Rather, the intercessor is someone who has entered a battle, the greatest battle of all between the powers of darkness and the hosts of the Most High God. I know I am in a fight and I have to be prepared for enemy onslaughts and wounds, but also for mighty victories too!

Thus an intercessor is someone to whom God's work has not just become important but paramount. That is why Jesus said "I *must* be about My Father's business." There is much value in trying to get a grip of the great prayer patterns of Moses, David, Jeremiah, Nehemiah, Ezra, Paul, Peter and Jesus Himself. Like these heroes, we are then more able not just to pray down the blessings of God, but also to lay hold of His mighty power and to come against the powers of darkness, breaking their hold in His Name. Intercession is one of the most rewarding ministries, but there is a price to pay and it can be very costly. It is energetic and tiring, and you have to be prepared for it "… in season and out of season whether it is convenient or not." 2 Tim 4.2. If you have done this, you will know it to be true. It is not an easy option. Yes, it might be easy to talk *about* the Lord, but to talk *to* Him often, regularly and faithfully is another matter. If I had wanted a cushy life, doing my own thing, I certainly would not have agreed to this ministry. Since I seek adventure, I know I am on the right track! Having taken on this challenge to stand in the gap, I needed to channel my aims, desires and hopes ever more on the living God. My ambitions and lifestyle had to be changed still further, which was not only costly time-wise, but involved foregoing some pleasures, quite innocuous in themselves such as friendships and music and other recreations that I had always assumed were my rights. Also sleep and food had to be under His discipline. With this ministry everything becomes subsidiary to God's holy calling.

Intercessors might be considered weird or fanatical, for instance by needing to retire to bed early in order to get up for that vital, early, unhurried quiet time, set aside for feeding on God's Word and speaking to Him. I have had to die to my reputation over this particular point, relinquish what others think of me and "count all things but loss for the excellency of the knowledge of Jesus Christ my Lord." Phil 3.8. I have found I need to be much more yielded, surrendered and submitted to the Lord as clay in His hands, and constantly filled afresh with the invigorating power of the Holy Spirit. Most of all I have realised that I need to keep a *soft* heart; a tender heart that sees what God sees, that feels what God feels and that somehow begins to comprehend something of His pain for the world He created. In large black letters, I wrote these words on our vicarage kitchen chimney breast; KEEP A SOFT HEART. They remained there for years and have been indelibly printed on my heart, and I pray on the hearts of the many who came into that room.

The standard is high, but how else will we climb? It might seem impossible for mere human beings to achieve anything or change anything in this broken world of ours, but this is not so with a God who "hears our cry and answers our prayer." Ps 116.1. He is mightier than the mightiest. He is more powerful than the most powerful and He is greater than the greatest, for HE IS GOD – THE ALMIGHTY GOD. And this, our God, tells us in Ezekiel 22.30 tells, that "I sought for a man, someone to make up the hedge and stand in the gap before Me, but found none". He was looking, longing and yearning for someone to intercede, but He found no one, not *one* person … how terribly sad. He is still looking today for people He can trust to do this work. Will He find a response I wonder? I do hope so. Amen.

## Father, is there anyone? (Jesus, talking to His Father)

*Father, is there anyone who'll join me as I pray -*
*One whose heart is meek and soft and with Me longs to stay?*
*Father, is there anyone who now will on Me wait –*
*Listen carefully to My voice, because the time is late?*
*Father, is there anyone to whom the world means naught –*
*Compared with heavenly treasures which My blood has bought?*
*Father, is there anyone who'll trembling come to Me –*
*With their face flat on the ground and in expectancy?*
*Father, is there anyone who'll step outside the camp –*
*Sharing My reproach, that they may bear My holy stamp?*
*Father, is there anyone who'll comprehend My grief –*
*For my bride who's slumbering, their times with Me but brief?*
*Father, is there anyone, O, is there anyone –*
*Who loves Me so intensely, My love their heart has won?*

# The scarlet thread

# CHAPTER 23

"A thread of scarlet." Song of Solomon 4.3

I wonder what this chapter title evokes in your mind? For me it speaks of a theme that runs right through the Bible from one end to the other like an unbroken scarlet thread. It is the theme of voluntary suffering for God etched in the blood of the prophets, the apostles and above all Jesus Christ. The thread demonstrates the inevitability of persecution of some kind for all those who follow Him wholeheartedly. In the west we are aware of the many Christians in other parts of the world suffering deprivation, arrest, imprisonment, torture and even death today, for love of their Saviour. It seems to me that we are almost *content* for this to be so, as long as it does not touch us personally. But if we are prepared to go the whole way with Him, it most certainly will.

We tend to ignore the many scriptures that show us this truth plainly and the important link between persecution and glory. Jesus told us in the Sermon on the Mount in Matt 5 .10 "Blessed are those who are persecuted for righteousness sake, for theirs is the kingdom of heaven." Peter told us in 1 Pet 4.14 "If we are reproached for the Name of Christ, we are happy, for the spirit of glory and of God rests on us." And Paul told us in 2 Tim 3.12 "All those who desire to live a godly life in Christ Jesus *will* suffer persecution." Jesus warns us in John 15.20 "if they have persecuted Me, they *will* persecute you also." And that includes religious leaders, see John 16.2. I labour this point because I have found it all too faintly comprehended.

When I first came to know the Lord Jesus, although I obviously did not know the Scriptures as well as I do now, I had found "the pearl of great price" Matt 13.46. There was "a spring in my step and a song in my mouth." (Billy Graham) and the Lord graciously kept me from any kind of persecution until I was well established in Him. This was not to last for long however, for within a year my mother informed me that she did not want me to come home for the university vacations. The rejection I experienced was inexplicably painful. I was just getting to know Tony at this point and he was the senior student at his theological college, whereas I was a mere 'nobody' at mine. What would he think if I told him that my mother, a vicar's wife no less, was refusing to allow her daughter to come home? I have to say that I was exceedingly anxious that this might put an early end to our relationship. I asked Barbara Johnston, one of my flat mates, who later became a missionary in South America, to talk to Tony on his next visit. I needed her to explain the situation with the knowledge she had of my credentials as a Christian and she duly performed this task. Thankfully Tony, still a young Christian, accepted her explanation. Mother relented pretty quickly and so I was only banned from coming home for one vacation.

My mother's problem stemmed from her upbringing in

a Bible believing home where servants were not treated as equals with the family. This inequality and snobbishness riled her and put her off evangelicals. Now to compound the problem, her daughter had become one whereas she had embraced **modernism** and this was the issue here. This was my first taste of persecution and being such a gentle trainer, the Lord let me in gradually, but it was not to be the only time I faced rejection. When Barbara left our flat to go to Bible College I could sense something was brewing. I was now 'de trop.' We were living in a flat in a house belonging to a Prima Donna singer who was a great friend of Kathleen Ferrier. The two other girls, who I do not believe were born again Christians, wanted their own friends to take the place of Barbara and I. In order to get rid of me they persuaded this landlady that I was dirty and untidy. This was untrue as I was in fact quite the opposite; meticulously fastidious, and still am!' For the second time I was thrown out. The problem here was **expediency**.

A long time ago, we were having a holiday in a missionary retreat in a beautiful setting with acres of land, and above all wonderful peace and quiet. There was a well used chapel and each evening a service was held and a message delivered. On one such evening, to my horror, a statue of Buddha appeared, and the aim of the message was to commend him. I and some others there were appalled and so I, as the 'ring leader', suggested that a prayer meeting should be held as soon as possible. It was agreed, and we met in one of the sitting rooms, having been given permission to do so. However there was an informer present, indeed a member of one of Tony's previous congregations. We prayed against the powers of darkness. We beseeched the Lord that this image be removed and that there be repentance and a turning back to the one and only true God. The following morning, Tony was summoned and told that my behaviour could no longer be tolerated and that we must leave immediately. This was a particularly restful place and one that we had often used for refreshing after the busyness of parish life and would sorely miss. The underlying problem here was clearly **idolatry,** which I felt must be challenged. We are told in Eph 5.11 "Have no fellowship with the works of darkness, but rather expose them."

In our retirement we tried out various churches, and in one of them I attended a ladies bible study held in the minister's house once a week. Very little was mentioned about the Bible, but there was a lot of New Age discussion. During one such meeting, I mentioned that one of my chief evangelistic opportunities was at the swimming club. One of the ladies said to me, "Do you not think they were Christians then?" I answered, "Of course this is likely to be the case, for anywhere you go you are bound to meet people who have no personal knowledge of the Lord Jesus." This made her laugh and so I asked her what had caused such a response, but there was no reply. Then everyone else started laughing too and in my amazement, I asked them, "Why do you find this so amusing?" Yet again there was no answer and a crescendo of laughing erupted. I was utterly baffled and could not believe that at a Bible study there should be, not only a complete lack of understanding of the need for evangelism, but that at the mention of this there should be such mockery. At the next meeting I was the last to arrive and whereas usually someone would kindly collect my special disabled chair from my car, this time nobody offered. All the seats were occupied and not one able bodied person volunteered to vacate theirs for me. For a while I had nowhere to sit, except uncomfortably on the floor. After that meeting, I was constrained to speak to the minister's wife about what had occurred at both meetings and she told me that she felt nothing at all was amiss! I then realised I was not wanted, so Tony and I felt that there was no point continuing at the church. The problem here was **universalism.**

Another sad situation arose from a similarly unlikely source several years ago, when we were hoping to settle into a new church. I became involved with a Bible study group and endeavoured both to receive and to contribute. A recurrent theme linking several important principles seemed either to be overlooked or not really understood. I felt I should not hold back for fear of unpopularity and therefore drew their attention to the relevant scriptures, asking how they should practically apply to our lives, but there was little response. They believed in the need for integration with the community in order to communicate the Gospel, but I sensed an increasing antagonism to the Lord's unchanging challenge also for separation; a distinctly different life style in today's world, which is increasingly ignorant of God's holiness.

There came a day when I was faced with a dilemma; one of my children really needed me, but it conflicted with the next Bible study which I dare not miss. I ventured to this meeting with an in depth study of the passage, much prayer and considerable trembling. I had come to love those dear people and longed for them to receive the greater blessings promised to those who are willing to obey God's world unreservedly. I expected opposition and I certainly got it.

Two days later the minister arrived at our home unannounced, clearly angry and upset. He lectured me for over half an hour with Tony present. He read 1 Corinthians 13 and then told me I was the very opposite. He described me as unkind and unloving. He told me I was the worst member of any congregation he had pastured. He pinned on me 'a kind of legalism which strips the cross of its power and had undermined the assurance of salvation in his precious flock.' He even pronounced a punishment; something he said that he had never done before, which we both felt would not be conducive to our usefulness there. I listened in stunned silence. Somehow I felt sorry for him. After he finished speaking, with tears in my eyes, I prayed a prayer of repentance for any lack of love I had unwittingly shown. I am sure he believed that he was righteously angry and because he is a God fearing man he will have taken it to the Lord, who alone sees the motives of all our hearts. As he left I gave him a kiss and said, 'May the peace of our Lord Jesus be upon you.' But after all this Tony felt it would be impossible to continue in that church. I think the underlying problem here was **worldliness**.

Before this contretemps I was training to be a Lay Reader at another church. The course usually takes four to five years on a part time basis, but the diocese had allowed me and a handful of others, including the head of

ACAS to do it in one year. I therefore worked tirelessly full time for this period, completing the reading required, the essays, the lectures and a huge time consuming profile of the church and parish. I kept as low a stance as I possibly could, but as part of my preparation I had to preach several times.

## St. Mary's – a poem I wrote for my profile

*So fine and independent now she stands*
*In valley green not wrought with human hands.*
*Reminder eloquent of ancient days;*
*Some secrets hidden, others yet portrays.*
*So beautiful in sunlit summer's eve,*
*Her spire towards heaven reaching, clouds receive.*
*Around her, sheep stand grazing in the field*
*In this fair Kentish countryside and weald.*

*Through plague she solitary stood for years.*
*The cost in human lives unnumbered. Tears*
*That spilled into the night of silent dreams.*
*But now, her shadow falls, or so it seems*
*Upon a cluster of warm dwellings, bent*
*On comforting this lonely Maid of Kent.*
*Her bells toll out again to human kind,*
*And in her solace, peace and love they find.*

A couple of weeks before I was due to be licensed and looking forward to the big day, one of the church wardens approached me and told me he wanted to see me after the service. The Lord then warned me that something was wrong, so I took Tony with me to see him. He requested that I should 'tone down' my preaching. This was odd considering his previous comments of approval and my preaching tutor's commendations. I replied as humbly as I could, that I sought the Lord for the messages I was to deliver and that I was not going to preach out of fear or for favour. He then mentioned that I needed another year's training, which was untrue and confirmed as unnecessary by the diocese. I realised then which side my bread was buttered! What transpired was that the previous vicar had shifted his evangelical position to a more liberal one. I can remember him telling me the reason for this before his departure; that being a conservative evangelical incurred too much opposition. This churchwarden had obviously contacted him and together they plotted the termination of my candidacy. I believe letters were passed to and fro and certainly one of them came into the hands of the other church warden. He offered me this letter which would have revealed the truth and vindicated me, but I refused to accept or use this to defend myself.

I then went to the diocesan head quarters to see my tutors and was told that only one other person, a woman, had ever been prevented from being licensed as a Lay Reader having completed the course. She had gone ballistic and they were curious to know why I had not! They were extremely sympathetic, but I told them it was a *'fait accompli.'* Furthermore I revealed to my tutors how I had at first wept for about twenty four hours, how I then turned to the Lord in my sorrow and how He had taken me up into the heavenlies and showed me that this was His doing and this was His sovereign will. I then shared the joy that He had placed in my heart, which was humanly inexplicable. Marvellous are the workings and ways of the Lord! The senior Lay Reader in the country (who happened to be one of my tutors) later wrote to me and told me that if any church would like to use me, he would be glad to arrange for me to be licensed. However, I now knew the Lord's sovereign will and declined, saying that I had no desire to proceed further. Instead I sought the Lord's face even more and was greatly blessed by reading Andrew Murray's book called Humility, which I then re-read another six times! The underlying problem here was **liberalism**. The last strand of scarlet thread and definitely the most devastating I have not included here. It is left for the next chapter on 'Brushes with the law' where the underlying problem was **occultic** and involved freemasonry.

Through all these trials, and there have been others for which there is no space or which I cannot expose, I can honestly say I have been wonderfully blessed by our gracious Heavenly Father and by His infallible Word. He has been my shield and defence and unfailing in His faithfulness. He told me not to fret, but to trust in Him, to delight in Him, to commit my way to Him, to wait patiently for Him and to rest in Him. (Ps 37) As I did this, I found the rejection I experienced in these situations only increased my consciousness of the acceptance of my Heavenly Father, for it drove me to Him. I came to understand that this was the disciplining of the Lord for His child so that I could better become "a partaker of His holiness and yield the fruit of righteousness." Heb 12.10, 11. I discovered from 1 Thes 3.3 that we should not be even be *moved* by these afflictions, because they have been appointed and planned by God Himself for our good.

When I reflect on Jesus life, a man of sorrows and acquainted with grief, the holy Son of God, who went about doing good, yet endured the fiercest opposition ever encountered, I see such a humble patient reaction compared with my own. And as I meditate on Jesus and see Him portrayed mainly by the religious leaders of His day, as mad, drunk and even demon possessed, I am even more astounded. He was misunderstood, un-thanked, despised, mocked, reproached, reviled, rejected, hated, betrayed, beaten and finally crucified. And He did all this for me, even me. Should I not bear just a chip of the cross of my wonderful Saviour?

Footnote: See Songs 4.3 "Thus all we do must be washed in the blood of Jesus and dyed with the scarlet thread." (Matthew Henry) The scarlet thread I believe speaks of the shed blood of Jesus and His voluntary willingness to suffer. As with the prophets before Him and the Apostles after Him, we must be willing for this suffering too. One day it will reveal whether we have the spiritual health and the beauty of His glory, as did the Shulamite's scarlet lips.

## His grief

*What grief like Yours for sinful man,*
*A grief that we can scarce believe*
*With all its ghastly agony.*
*Its scarlet thread defines Your plan.*
*A grief inside that few receive,*
*A grief that must touch you and me.*

*Unless we comprehend this grief*
*The Word we casually impart*
*To mind and soul, with little cost,*
*And time with Him is only brief.*
*We'll never understand God's heart*
*We'll never go to win the lost.*

*Unless we learn to weep and pray*
*And watch and wait; by Him be told,*
*Unless we feel God's agony,*
*And long all day with Him to stay,*
*Unless His grief we grasp and hold*
*Our lives will surely shallow be.*

# Brushes with the law

"You will be brought before rulers ... for My Name's sake ... settle it therefore in your hearts not to consider before what you shall answer, for I will give you a mouth and wisdom." Luke 21.14,15

Worse was to come; new spectres appeared from seemingly nowhere, which I had never had to tackle before and which I could have avoided, but for the fact that I had one goal, whatever the cost. I now had to confront evil in high places.

The first was when some friend s of mine who had sons at a boarding school shared with me from time to time their concern about a homosexual housemaster who was abusing his position and causing the boys stress. Eventually two or three of these women came to see me and asked if I could do anything to help. I prayed long and hard about this, not wanting to get entangled, yet seeing the anxiety it engendered. I shared all this with Tony who wanted no part in this himself as he thought we would be unable to spell out precisely what the master had done, without risk of litigation. However, he gave me this freedom. Eventually I decided that if no one else dared, I must be willing to face the headmaster with what I now felt to be fact. The headmaster came to see me in our home and kept asking, 'Is Mr. X harassing the boys with homosexuality?' My answer was, 'I hear you say so.' These words I learned from my mother for use in difficult situations. Many times he repeated the same question and every time I gave him the same answer. He did indeed threaten me with litigation and when he left I shook with fear, for I knew nothing about the law, yet was certain I had once more to 'expose the works of darkness'.

Thankfully, because this school has a high reputation for integrity and morality, the master in question was immediately demoted from being a house master and after the end of term was never seen again. I waited nervously and with a horrible foreboding that something would happen that might implicate me, but nothing ever did. The headmaster left to go to another school and I never saw him again until several years later, when I spotted him walking towards me in town. He had a very striking face which could not easily be missed. I approached him cautiously, and surprisingly he remembered me when I spoke to him; and also what had transpired all those years ago. Quickly he said these few words, 'You were right in what you silently implied.' Then, with a twinkle in his eye he added, 'I knew!'

A similar situation developed with a girl whom I knew well. She was a member of our Young People's Fellowship and someone I had helped with interview technique. She was also a medical student doing her 2nd M.B. course. She came to see me, very upset, because a member of the academic staff was interfering with the female students during practical physiology and she was seriously thinking of quitting medicine. I felt it incumbent on me to try to do something about this to help her and all the others affected. With much prayer and not a little trepidation I ventured forth to the hospital concerned and the first person I met of any significance was one of the professors, to whom I spilled the beans and he asked for my name and address. I then met up with other students who confirmed that this practice was indeed going on. I was also told of a former student, who I believe had left on account of this. I visited her and she told me the same story. Not so long after this I received a letter from the Dean of the medical school warning of impending litigation. I was now terrified and it seemed there was no one to help me, that is, no human being. Just imagine the scenario; the Dean, the whole medical school staff and the hospital dignitaries coming against one hopelessly naïve woman!

A well known minister encouraged me to expose this in the Daily Telegraph, but I decided against his advice. However, a young doctor from the same hospital arrived in our church, assured me this practice was happening and he himself continued the crusade. This brave doctor stepped into the arena willingly and the upshot was that never again was this man allowed to be with the female students during physiology practicals. The girl stayed on and qualified as a doctor. For a long time I had a dread of being hauled to court and finding myself without a leg to stand on. I had to learn from these experiences that my trust must be totally rooted in the Lord, who would protect me, even if the worst happened. And as you can see, He did just that. Praise His name!

Even worse was to come, which could have affected Tony's whole ministry and left him without a job, house or pension. He was pastoring a large church where at first it seemed we were idolized, then criticized, then scandalised and finally largely ostracized. We went from hero to zero in a matter of two years. From out of the blue, or so it seemed, a storm suddenly arose; a storm of opposition to both Tony and me. I had just started a youth fellowship in our house which had become large and full of vigour. We were anxious that these young people should not become involved and then hurt.

Tony's preaching had hit a very sore spot; he had shown his disapproval of Freemasonry during a teaching series on the occult. What we were completely unaware of was that some of the church leaders and several members of the congregation were freemasons. We were unfamiliar with the history of this church and the fact that annual freemasonry services had been held there for many years after it was built in 1875. Every vicar had had problems. Clifford Hill came to our church not knowing any of this and warned against freemasonry and forthwith nine men walked out, thereby I believe, identifying themselves.

Many complaints began to surface via the letter box or by phone. Mysterious lies began to circulate through the congregation, which is not surprising as the devil is the father of lies. There were even threats that we might be sued, but for what we had no idea. Tony was portrayed as unsound in his theology and that he was undermining the atonement, when nothing could have been further from the truth! Some said he was weak while others said he was too dominating, and as it is not possible to be both, I guess he got it just right and stood somewhere in between! The allegations against me were even worse. I heard the shocking word 'nymphomaniac' used to descibe me. They said I was doing the devil's work when I prayed with and counselled people, because they presumed I had divulged the secrets I heard. In fact I never once did, not even to Tony. They were sceptical about my laying hands on the sick in spite of the fact that some were healed and remained in the church. Perhaps even more scandalous was the fact that I, as a woman, actually preached in church, being neither a Lay Reader nor having been ordained.

Those who were opposed continued to put the knife in and tried to get us out. The next accusation was that I had tried to push one of the church wardens into the busy main road traffic. This would have been impossible, for he was quite a large man and I a small woman. Yet another accusation was that Tony had attempted to rig the ballot for the election of church wardens at the annual church meeting. Eventually some of the leaders approached the Bishop and a meeting similar to a consistory court, was convened. Nine church leaders were on one side, Tony and two new godly churchwardens who had just been elected were on the other, and the Bishop and Archdeacon adjudicated. I was tried in my absence. Soon after this, the Bishop ordered us both to come and see him immediately. Noel Atkins, who had been a former church warden and who was now living in Denmark, heard of our plight and he very kindly typed a letter, which he duplicated and sent to the Bishop, Archbishop and ourselves. This was the main thrust of the letter:

"May I propose that if the present position is not satisfactorily resolved forthwith to the satisfaction of the Reverend and Mrs. March, then the British legal system be invoked. That through the searches of a lawyer an Industrial Tribunal be convened consisting of no freemasons. This would allow a fair trial of the matter in hand at which I should be glad to attend. As, Sir, I do not know your personal position on the subject of freemasonry, but I find it unusual that you have declined the reasonable request of Tony and Gillian March to discuss the matter … I am taking the opportunity of forwarding a copy of this letter to the present Archbishop of Canterbury, Dr Robert Runcie, who I know is not a freemason. There is no need to mention the love, devotion and impeccable Christian testimony of Tony and Gillian because these facts stand for themselves and are plain to be seen by any sane minded person, whether he be a Christian or not …Noel Atkins RD, Lieutenant Commander Rtd.

An audience with the Bishop was delayed by two weeks, for immediately the letter arrived his secretary rang to say that he was indisposed. When we finally appeared before his Lordship, he spent what seemed half the time asking the same question, "Is it a matter of freemasonry?" Tony said nothing. I said as I had before with the headmaster, "I hear you say so, my Lord." Eventually the Bishop revealed that all his family were freemasons, though he never divulged the secret that he was one too. After this meeting the Archdeacon came and told us that we were exonerated and that we could stay at the church until Tony was seventy! He then came to the Parochial Church Council and gave them a piece of his mind! By this time, the onslaughts of the freemasons and those they had influenced had precipitated a serious nervous breakdown in Tony. This took him about three years from which to completely recover and he was virtually off work for the best part of a year. This nightmare God used for good, for it gave him greater understanding and more ability to minister to those who are in this dark tunnel. It was a nightmare experience for me too, as I battled to instil some sort of normality and routine into our lives, and through this harrowing experience the Lord taught me a tremendous amount. Earlier I had written a letter to the Bishop. I did not admit that I was guilty of the alleged crimes for they were not true; however I said that I was indeed a sinner, but that I had been saved by the precious blood of Jesus. I sought in this way to present the gospel to him and I begged his forgiveness for any disruption I had caused in the parish. The letter was four foolscap pages long and I wonder whether he was flabbergasted?

I cannot end this chapter without telling you another story which is connected with the last. Some time later I was taken to Freemason's Hall in Great Queen's Street London to hear a debate between a Christian and a freemason. At this debate was a person who kept a record of all known freemasons in the Church of England. I asked him if our Bishop was one and he replied, "We think he is, but we cannot be absolutely certain." Weeks later, I was parking my car in a spot that I was not quite certain was permitted. There I saw another man parking and I went up to him and asked him if I was parked legally, to which he replied, "Yes." Seeing a black case in his hand I asked him "Are you a doctor? "No, I'm on the way to my lodge." he answered. Straight out of my mouth, without a moments thought, and no previous knowledge I said, "Then you will know the Bishop" and he responded, "I do indeed. He is a member of our lodge." This is how I discovered that our Bishop was a freemason!

The Lord will impart to us through His gifts, exactly what He thinks we should know. How wonderfully true that when we are brought before rulers or *bishops*, if we rely totally on Him, He will give us the words to speak and He will impart His wisdom. Furthermore, He will be a rock of defence, our hiding place and our deliverer, for He is exactly what He promises to be – the Faithful One.

# A tough assignment

# CHAPTER 25

"The Lord said, 'Do not be afraid of their words or dismayed by their looks. You shall speak My Words to them, whether they hear or whether they refuse.'"
Ezekiel 2.6, 7

There is nothing more difficult or more challenging than to be called into the Prophetic Ministry, especially if one is a woman, yet this was indeed part of God's calling on my life and those who knew me well also discerned that this was the case, including the head of YWAM in this country. The Lord had already spoken to me powerfully by bringing my attention to Isaiah 41. 15 "Behold I will make you into a new threshing instrument with sharp teeth." But now I realised that the Lord was requiring me to personally accept and obey this scripture. I did not relish the thought at all; in fact I positively quaked at the very idea. I knew that those called into this ministry have never been popular in the world or even in the church and never will be. A prophet's lot is to be misunderstood, silenced or in some manner slain.

To encourage me, the Lord gave me several public prophecies which I delivered when doing the intercessions in our church which were surprisingly well received. Then one day, soon after the 2004 Tsunami, I was in the garden and I heard the Lord speaking to me and telling me that I needed to write something down. I went into the house and fetched pen and paper and then with my mind almost in suspense, the words literally rolled onto the paper, and this is the prophecy He gave me.

*"O My people hear what the sovereign Lord says; the peoples of this world think there has been a terrible natural disaster. They call it 'nature,' but nature is not My Name. My Name is Jehovah, the Lord God Almighty. I have spoken and My voice has echoed throughout the world. I am the Lord of glory, who thunders through the skies. My voice is so powerful and so full of majesty that it breaks the trees, it shakes the mountains, and it resounds through the deserts. When I speak, My voice sounds forth so that the earth trembles and the waves roar. Listen to Me. I am the God of the universe. I am God of the earth. I am the God of the seas. Few listen to My voice. I weep that so few listen even though I sent My Son to be the Saviour of the world, the One whose birth you have just celebrated. Now I sound forth yet again through My prophets; I have spoken through many lesser judgments, to warn, but few have heeded My voice. I speak now both in My wrath and in My love and compassion. I speak to show My world that I am the Sovereign God who reigns, the Almighty Everlasting God and the One with whom you have to do. This latest judgment is one of those I promised to send in the last days. I yearn that you, My people, will take heed to this judgment.*

*I have a contention with those I have created; first with the nations of the East who have many other gods; to whom they give names, who they call gods, and worship as if they were true gods, but there is only one God and I am He. Then with the nations of the West, who also have their gods, though they do not recognise them as gods; gods of materialism and hedonism. They live luxuriously while others have little food or water. These gods they worship, so they cannot worship Me.*

But my main contention is with My Church; whom I bought with the most precious blood of My Son, the Lord Jesus Christ. A few of My saints will dare to suffer, to have their possessions confiscated, to be hounded and put in dungeons, to be tortured and killed for the love of Me – and these are largely not in the West. Yet you Western Christians, surfeited with luxuries will not speak even a word for Me for fear, where there is almost no persecution. You will not open your mouth for fear of man, where there is democracy, while countless perish eternally for lack of knowing Me. Your knowledge of Me is skin deep. You say you worship Me but your heart is far from Me. While millions pass into a godless eternity, you still revel in your parties. You drank wine and ate exotic foods and continued feasting knowing that thousands were being overwhelmed by My raging seas, as if nothing terrible had happened.

I am weeping, for I hate to send My judgments. I love to stretch forth My hand and save and bless. I am grieved that the people I have created are passing into everlasting hell for lack of knowing who I am and not turning to Me for Salvation. My church, My precious bride is lured to sleep. She is intoxicated with self indulgence. You say that you know Me. You say that you love Me. You say I am your God. Am I really? Your god is the one whom you think about the most. Are your minds filled with thoughts of Me, or are they filled with vain imaginations, selfish plans, and proud ideas? Will any of My people weep with Me? Will any share My grief? Will any rend themselves in sackcloth and ashes? Will any fast and pray?

This judgment I have had to send upon the guilty and the innocent will affect you all, for the whole world lies under My judgment.

*No one will escape the effects of these recent happenings. Some complacent rich ones will ride out the storm, but only temporarily. They already have their reward here and will forfeit it hereafter. Wake up Church. The time is short. My voice has shaken the world. Yet once more will I shake not only the earth and sea, but the heavens also. Understand, My redeemed ones that this judgment is to tell you, to remind you, as if this were necessary, that I AM COMING AND I AM COMING VERY SOON. And you will see me coming on the clouds, and every eye will see Me, even those who pierced Me. The whole world will mourn because of Me. But you, My children, you who have loved Me and are following Me, look up and rejoice for behold your redemption draws near. So be prepared. Behave like men. Trim your lamps, prepare your hearts, wash and be cleansed and put away the evil from before My eyes. I see everything. I know what is in your heart. You have forsaken me your Lord. You have provoked me to anger; the Holy One of Israel. You have turned backwards.*

*For this is what the High and lofty One who inhabits eternity and whose Name is Holy, says; I dwell in the high and holy place, with him who has a contrite heart and a humble spirit. I am Holy, so be you holy, for without holiness no man shall see the Lord. And prepare a way for Me, your Lord. Make My paths straight. Make My way known. Make a highway for your God. For I am the God of Glory, so prepare yourselves now before it is too late and you too are overwhelmed. Be READY. Behold, I come quickly.”* Even so come Lord Jesus. Amen.

Far more than just giving words of prophecy, this ministry involves listening carefully to what the Lord is saying at a certain time and in a given situation and then correctly interpreting it. The response now is vital, “to speak whether they hear or forbear.” Ezek 3.11. This can be to a group of people or to an individual. How necessary is Isaiah 50.4 "The Lord God has given me the tongue of the wise, that I should know how to speak a word in season." How does He do this? Verse 5 tells us, "He wakens us morning by morning. He awakens my ear to hear." The greatest need in the prophetic ministry therefore is first to listen to the Lord and then do what He says and say what He says, whatever the cost. In Jer 1.7, 8 He instructs by these words; "Do not say I am too young (or too old); for you shall go to all to whom I send you. And whatever I command you, you shall speak. Do not be afraid ... for I am with you to deliver you." There will be a price to pay sooner or later. There is often misunderstanding of the prophetic ministry along with criticism and even outright hostility. As Stephen said, "Which of the prophets have you not persecuted?" Acts 7.52.

In His mercy and grace the Lord knows how to uphold His servants in wonderful ways. He draws their attention to relevant parts of His Word which saves them from becoming utterly cast down. As in Jeremiah 1.8 and also Psalm 23.3 "He restores my soul and leads me in the paths of righteousness for His Name's sake." I am sure that everyone who has been appointed to this ministry feels reluctant, as I did and still do. Sometimes I wish I could fly away like a dove, or hide under a rock or just be allowed to keep my mouth shut! I am sure I often fail in this ministry and also that I often get it wrong, but the Lord tells me to continue in the calling into which He has called me, and so I must obey; hence this poem.

## Will you warn?

*Lord, I'm grieved I have not always been*
*That burning firebrand You desired,*
*Nor threshing instrument, so keen*
*And sharp, and never growing tired.*

*Lord, I'm sorry I've preferred the praise*
*Of men, than speak, exhort and warn,*
*And thus Your righteous standards raise.*
*My cowardice I truly mourn.*

*Lord, help me Your blessed path to choose,*
*Agree, relinquish my own way,*
*And Your enablings for me use,*
*In Your assignment gladly stay.*

*Lord, set my quaking heart on fire,*
*And bend the centre of my will*
*To rescue those in sin's deep mire*
*With Your own Word and heavenly skill*

*Lord, blow Your wind upon me now,*
*And fan the flames of ardent love*
*That cause me to obey, and bow*
*Before Your glorious throne above.*

# Amazing provisions

# CHAPTER 26

"Jehovah Jireh; the Lord will provide." Genesis 22.14

How can I begin to recount all the ways my Heavenly Father has provided for all my needs and more? They are beyond telling, for they are boundless and occur almost every day; sometimes in small ways and at other times in incredibly big ways. Nevertheless, I will try to convey some of the most significant provisions I can remember, from the least to the greatest.

When setting up home, the first consideration after obtaining accommodation is acquiring furniture. Most people have to buy their own, but we were so grateful for the many people who supplied most of ours over the years. In retirement to a small cottage, we realised that our three piece suite could in no way be squeezed into our tiny sitting room! We went off to order our very first brand new one and put down a deposit of five hundred pounds, the balance being two thousand pounds. On returning home, there on the front door mat was an envelope with a legacy from Agnes Brownlow, one of our kind friends from the church, and in this envelope was exactly two thousand pounds!

For the first five years of our marriage and with three children, we had no car and felt that we really needed one.

We bought second hand cars for about ten years and our last model, an old Ford Anglia kept breaking down and finally became marooned in London. At this stage we were living in Tunbridge Wells and for the third time Tony was up in the city trying to sort it out. The phone rang and the matron of the Aged Pilgrims Home asked me whether Tony could come and take a service there the following week which was Easter week, the busiest in the church's calendar. Ever since the car broke down, Tony had been using our daughter Rachel's bike to get around our very large parish and much time was taken up cycling to and fro; visiting parishioners, attending meetings and taking services. I therefore hesitated before telling her about Tony's predicament, but then of course agreed on his behalf. When Tony arrived at the home to take the service, a lady answered the door and handed him an envelope. When he opened it, there inside was one thousand pounds! We sold the old Ford for one hundred pounds and bought our first brand new car, an Avenger Estate, for exactly one thousand, one hundred pounds!

The cost of Rachel's education as I mentioned earlier was amazingly provided by our loving Heavenly Father. Similarly, we felt Andrew needed better education than he was getting at his state primary school. We could not possibly afford the fees of the prep school to which we hoped to send him, but nevertheless, I rang the Headmaster and asked to see him regarding a place at his school. I also explained our financial circumstances. "There are no spaces here anyway," he replied. Then without really thinking I murmured pensively, "What a pity." Sensing my great disappointment he lingered on the phone and I found myself telling him that my husband went to Haileybury, my father to Charterhouse and my brother to Marlborough. "Come and see me at eleven o'clock tomorrow," he snapped.

I took Andrew the following morning, armed with football boots (because he was good at sports), poems he had written, pictures he had painted, his music case and his violin. During the interview Andrew was called out to be auditioned by the senior music master. He sang, played the piano and the violin. After this there was a 'pow-wow' and then we were called back to the Headmaster's office. He told us "there is a space for Andrew and we have created a new scholarship; a music scholarship. We will also give him an academic scholarship, both of which will cover the fees for one term each year. We returned home jubilant, but now we had to find the fees for the second term, as we could only, with great difficulty, manage the third. My father helped us by very generously paying for this.

When it came to secondary education, the fees at any public school were prohibitive and Andrew had not been prepared for the eleven plus examination at his prep school, as an assumption was made that pupils will continue along the private route. But here my brother Dick Marcon came up trumps. Being a Liveryman of the Fishmonger's Guild, he knew that they were prepared to educate one boy at a time at Christ's Hospital. It so happened that the next boy had not yet been selected and Dick managed to persuade them of Andrew's need and prowess. He was thus put forward, was accepted and then went on to pass the entrance examination. During the seven years he spent there, all his tuition, food, clothing, music lessons and travelling expenses were totally covered, so that we never paid a single penny!

Each summer the Lord supplied us with holidays through various people; Sometimes it was at our parent's homes, other times at relatives and quite often we were given holidays in Cornwall or Wales and one year, the New Forest. Not only were British holidays provided, but besides the Hawaiian Sabbatical, others abroad too. We were regularly invited to Switzerland by our friends John and Gisela McGowan, but actually only went on four occasions, staying in their house in Bissone on the edge of lake Lugano. Our friends Noel and Helena Atkins very kindly invited us to stay with them in Denmark at least three times. Also our friend Peter Carr invited us to Provence up in the Pre Alps one summer. When my sister was retiring as an air hostess from British Airways, she was given the opportunity of taking two people with her to the destination of her choice at only one tenth of the cost. I had been ill for some weeks with chest infections during the winter and so it was arranged that my father, Susan and I go to Africa, where I could get the sunshine I needed to recover and we could all have a great holiday together. Thus the Lord enabled me to have three weeks in Southern Africa and visit five countries; Uganda, Kenya, Southern Rhodesia and Zambia. I then went on to South Africa to stay with Tony's best man, Bruce Evans, who later became the Bishop of Port Elizabeth.

Four years before we retired, our younger daughter Sarah had renovated a Georgian cottage. As we needed a house for our retirement, we bought this from her. The cost of the house was a hundred and five thousand pounds, the legal cost five thousand and the creation of a garden also five thousand. At exactly this time the sum of one hundred and fifteen thousand pounds was left to us in my parents will!

Because of my many health problems in retirement, and being unable to walk hardly any distance, I have been awarded the Disability Living Allowance over the last fifteen years which we have commuted to Motability. This enables us to have a new Ford Focus every three years at no cost to us except for petrol. More recently with increasingly complex health issues, I have also been awarded the Top Care Allowance that practically covers all the extra medical expenses involved, and which have been considerable.

The supreme provision the Lord has given me in this world is my truly wonderful husband. He has been my lover, my friend, my soul-mate, my number one supporter, my confidant and my encourager. He is my spiritual rock, continually getting out the Word of God, and because he has a fund of Biblical knowledge at his finger tips, he is able to answer all my questions, pointing me to the exact passage I need and showing me how to interpret difficult Scriptures that appear abstruse. He not only knows the Word of God, but he lives it out, and this is evident to all.

Then there are my three beautiful, adorable children; Rachel, Sarah and Andrew. They all love and support me and have fellowship with me in our Lord Jesus Christ. I cannot thank the Lord enough for these marvellous human gifts. As I have received so much from the Lord, how generous I should be to Him and to those in need. We have always tithed our money, but the Lord showed me that deep down in my heart something was not quite right. There was something lurking there, a slight resentment and I was not giving as 2 Cor 9.7 tells us, "Let everyone give … not reluctantly or under compulsion, for God loves a cheerful giver." I once told my own father that there was an 'L' in his God (gold). As I was writing this I realised that I too had an 'L' in my God.

Our daughter Rachel is incredibly generous, although her husband has lost his job. Her example, together with the scriptures I had just read, convicted me and shed light on this important matter. As a result, I believe the Lord has broken this hold which the enemy had on my life. What a relief! Hence this poem which I wrote sometime ago but actually intended for someone else!

## Generous soul

*O generous soul, what wealth you do possess*
*In mind and heart, that others you may bless,*
*Especially those in life who have much less.*
*On them who owe you aught, you do not press*
*The pound of flesh, or cause them then distress.*
*You freely give; God's love you will express.*

*Yes generous soul; you've thrown your precious bread*
*On waters, and it will come back and spread*
*Like sweetest honey in your own homestead.*
*And with it you yourself be blessed and fed.*
*Your whole life through reveals this golden thread*
*Of open hand; by Him alone are led.*

*Why generous soul you for this beauty long?*
*The beauty of a hand stretched out, and strong*
*To help the ones in need, whom others wrong.*
*A character that gives and gives daylong,*

*Evokes a joyful spirit, given to song.*
*Your treasure is in heaven, where you belong.*

*Wise generous soul, you know that treasure sure*
*We never here on earth by wealth procure,*
*However much it's tempting power and lure.*
*You know that this world's gain is not the cure.*
*You've found time gone this makes the spirit poor,*
*Bereft of blessings that you could secure.*

*So generous soul, you give and give again.*
*You do not even feel the lack or pain,*
*For in God's Word He's made it very plain,*
*That those who give are freed from constant strain.*
*Your God, Jehovah Jireh, will maintain*
*Your lot; what's more – in heaven with Him you'll reign.*

How generous is our God! He has promised "To supply all our needs according to His riches in glory by Christ Jesus". The greatest provisions I have had or anyone can have, however, are not to be compared with the priceless gift of our Lord Jesus Christ Himself when He comes to be resident in our lives. He has shed His love upon me in incredible ways; I know "I am My Beloved's and He is mine and His banner over me is love." He has placed in my heart such "joy... which is my strength." He has imparted His peace "which passes all understanding". He has given me "the riches of full assurance". He has comforted me, for "He is the God of all comfort". For "with the Lord Jesus Christ, He freely gives us all things." And so I can cry out with the psalmist "whom have I in heaven or on earth that

I desire besides You?" There is none, for He has become everything to me. What more can any person desire?

## Giving thanks always

*We're sometimes sad that people fail*
*To render thanks. Response was due*
*When someone we have sought to bless*
*With gift we deemed of high value,*
*Yet recognition scarcely given.*
*It must be worthless in their view!*

*'Tis wonder more that blessings poured*
*Upon us mortals here; riches dug*
*From heaven's store, yet often spurned.*
*Lord, hearts so dull and cold unplug*
*To feel Your grief. Unvalued gifts*
*Passed off quite simply with a shrug.*

*A bounteous Saviour have we now*
*When eyes perceive Your generous way.*
*Great blessings piled upon our lives*
*To give us joy each passing day.*
*The blessing is God's blessed Son,*
*Who's come to bless and come to stay.*

*Lord, melt my heart to thank You more*
*For all the blessings showered on me,*
*Unnumbered special mercies shown,*
*In memory lost, I would not see?*
*Help me observe each single one*
*That truly thankful I might be.*

# A cat with nine lives

# CHAPTER 27

"My times are in Your hands." Psalm 31.15

I could have died many times, but like the cat, I have had nine lives! Why this should be so? I have no idea, but I guess the Lord has a lot of sanctification work to do in my life. Maybe He also wants me to reach some more people for the Kingdom. Or, could it be that He has been waiting for me to get down to writing this book? Odd scraps of my history have been sitting in a bottom drawer for years despite the fact that I have often been asked to write it. Three authors have offered to write it for me. One thing is certain, that as I have revisited my past and brought to memory so many different events, I have become increasingly aware, more so than ever before, of the Lord's goodness, love, mercy, patience, protection and grace in my life. In fact I am utterly amazed that He has taken this feeble and erring life and turned it round with such blessing. I am more profoundly grateful to Him now for all He has done for me, and been to me, as a result of writing this book.

The first of the nine lives was being born at all. My mother delivered my brother Dick three months prematurely, weighing only one and a half pounds. There were no incubators or modern technology, so she struggled to keep him alive, his life being in jeopardy for many months. When Dick was only seven months old, my mother conceived me. She told me herself years later, that it was not the right timing. There was no satisfactory contraception available in those days, nearly eighty years ago. Thus my mother used her own method every time she thought she might have an unplanned pregnancy; the instrument being a salt douche which hung in the bathroom, to my chagrin when my friends came to stay. All my childhood I was in fear of being poisoned and I believe it was because she had tried to abort me. If this is true, she did not succeed and I am profoundly grateful that the Lord gave me life.

The second cat's life was when I was eleven and living in Eastbourne. My father took me out on his motor bike with me riding pillion. He was visiting one or two parishioners who had contracted tuberculosis and were incarcerated in a sanatorium. We were on our way home; travelling down Langley Road at about thirty miles an hour and my father went straight across the Pevensey Road, not seeing a Ford V8 army lorry travelling at sixty miles per hour. Thus we crashed with a ninety mile an hour impact.

My father went straight over the handle bars, broke the back of his skull and lay unconscious for six weeks. It was only a miracle due to prayer that he recovered. I, on the other hand, was sent flying about thirty yards and up against a concrete wall. I too was unconscious for awhile and I remember when I was coming round someone saying "Are you a girl guide, because if you are, you won't cry?" I was taken to the same hospital as my father where they correctly diagnosed a broken leg, but failed to x-ray me for any spinal injury, which indeed I had sustained. Unbeknown to me, I had a huge gash on my ankle which was sewn up with indissoluble sutures over which was applied plaster of paris up to my knee. I was then put in a children's ward where gradually my temperature rose and I was told I could not go home after the two weeks planned initially. I decided to take the matter into my own hands; when the nurse put the thermometer in my mouth, I would tuck myself below the bedclothes and keep looking to see when the mercury reached 98.4 F. At that point I kept the thermometer between my teeth and not under my tongue. The nurses were surprised at the sudden drop in my temperature, but I was allowed to go home and I told my mother what I had done! My temperature continued to rise and my ankle itched so much that I was given a long knitting needle to scrape it, no record having been made of my lacerated ankle or the indissoluble sutures. Thus I developed septicemia which could easily have proved fatal, but again the Lord allowed me to recover.

The third cat's life was while I was at medical school. There was the worst smog ever recorded in this country and now known as the Great Smog of '52. Smog is fog mixed with smoke and produces highly pollutant air, which can cause health problems such as difficulty in breathing, reduced resistance to lung infections and eye irritation. I stupidly walked in this yellow 'Pea-Souper' across London to visit my friend Ann Morris, who was a student at the Royal College of Music. By the evening it was not possible to see one's outstretched hand and so we agreed that I should stay for the night. In the morning I felt ill and by the next evening extremely ill. I was admitted to hospital and put in a single ward. I remember a kind of canopy was put over me with a kettle boiling inside to help me breathe. I was given crystalline penicillin injections every four hours for two weeks and I gradually recovered. I had contracted a severe form of pneumonia and was told on leaving the ward that I had nearly lost my life. I survived but ten thousand others died in that London smog and many more suffered respiratory disorders for the rest of their lives, including myself.

The Lord pre-warned me about the fourth cat's life although I did not recognise this at the time. In the morning I was reading Isaiah 43 and was struck by verse 2. "When you pass through the waters I will be with you." I wrote at the top of my notebook the word 'waters.' That day Tony and I had been invited by an old school friend of his to join him for lunch at the Grand Hotel in Eastbourne. Afterwards we went to the beach, I for a swim, but not the two men. I spotted someone with a lilo and asked if I might borrow it. I was given permission on the condition I promised to bring it back. I happily floated out oblivious that a current was taking me further and further out to sea. When I realised my predicament I took fright. The sea was much rougher than I had noticed before, and in trying to hold on to the lilo I began to swallow water. I then realised I was drowning. I remembered the morning's Bible reading and cried out, "Lord, save me." Immediately, two men appeared from nowhere, with ropes around their waists. They approached me and helped me out of the sea. Then they said, "Did you not see the red flag warning no-one to swim?" I had not seen it and told them this. I clambered exhausted up the beach and slumped down beside Tony and his friend and gasped, "I nearly drowned, but two men came and saved me." Tony and his friend had seen nothing and as the wind was quite strong, neither had they heard my cry. I stood up after I had regained strength, to go and thank these men and walked up and down the beach asking people where I might find them, but no one had seen them. Finally someone told me, "There are no life-savers on the seaside at East-bourne." So I wonder whether the Lord had sent two angels, but I know that when I was sinking in the water, He was with me as He had promised.

The fifth cat's life I have described at length in the chapter headed 'Attempted Murder.' Here you will remember how, though my husband and I were viciously assaulted, the Lord spared our lives in a wonderful way. Likewise the sixth cat's life is recorded in the chapter entitled 'Feet' when I suffered a heart attack and how He totally healed me. Soon after this episode I was at a barbeque with David Chaput, a professor of medicine, and I described my symptoms, without mentioning the ambulance men's diagnosis. He said straight away, "You had a heart attack." The seventh cat's life was when we were about to retire. I was gradually getting increasingly more severe pain and numbness in my right leg. For months I was not diagnosed, despite seeing several doctors and being given physiotherapy. My daughter Sarah was suspicious and sent me to a doctor with whom she worked who in turn sent me immediately to see an orthopedic consultant. X-ray after X-ray showed nothing and it was not until Sarah demanded another one, that an oblique lumbar spinal X-ray told the tell tale signs of spinal infection revealing the danger I was in. The consultant had nearly given up and could have missed it. I was immediately admitted to hospital and put on four thousand milligrams of intravenous antibiotics and later continued with the same dose orally for six months. A solid spinal jacket was also made for me. My spinal cord was so stenosed in two places that seeing the MRI scans Sarah went as white as a sheet and told me I could very well have been paralysed from the waist down. I am blessed to have survived an illness which might so very nearly have been missed and cost me my life.

The last two cat's lives occurred in our retirement. Over a long period of my life I had frequent respiratory infections due to the smog, and therefore required frequent antibiotics. This led to a deficient immune system and I developed systemic candidiasis. I gradually lost three stone, being of a normal weight to start with, and then abdominal pain set in and I was eventually hospitalised. There I was given a gastroscopy where they discovered candida in the lower oesophagus, one lobe of my right lung had collapsed, later my foot became paralysed and a host of other problems presented themselves. My daughter Sarah came to visit me in hospital when I was asleep and she thought I was dead; I looked so ill. Also two of my consultants not involved with this particular problem of mine, but who regularly saw me, told me recently that they were convinced at the time that I had carcinomatosis and were amazed to see me still alive. No medical remedy was prescribed for the candidiasis and I grew weaker. It was not until my friend Mary Holden advised me about a good private clinic, that I received the right medication; large doses of Nystarin for a long time Many people from all over Europe attend this clinic for exactly the same reason that I did, as there is no NHS help provided for this condition unless the patient also has cancer or is HIV positive. The candida had spread to so many parts of my body that if I had not received the medical care of this clinic, I could have eventually died of disseminated candidiasis.

The ninth and last cat's life was very recent. I was showing symptoms of endocrine disorder, but again no medical help was forthcoming. I became profoundly fatigued so that I was unable to fulfill normal daily tasks. Once again it was Sarah, who not being able to bear it any longer, arranged for me to see an endocrinologist at the local hospital. There I was given blood tests at various intervals. On one occasion I rang to ask the exact time of my next appointment and was told by the secretary that the consultant was far too busy to see me and that I should make another appointment. I replied, "I've been given this appointment and I am going to keep it." I was given further blood tests at the appointment the following morning, after which I went off to Brighton for osteopathic treatment. On arrival home I received a frantic phone call from the consultant saying, "Get your husband to take you to your GP now. I have arranged for medication that is vital for your survival." My cortisol level had dropped dramatically from 750 nano molecules per litre to 26, and was fast approaching zero, at which point I would have gone into a coma. I had adrenal failure, for my pituitary gland had shrivelled up. My consultant kept in touch with Sarah and me over the next week and she told me I had had a very narrow escape and would not have survived for more than a few days, but for the intervention of the drug supplied.

I can honestly say that "For me to live is Christ and to die is gain" Phil 1.21 but for the present the Lord obviously wants me here on this earth, otherwise He would not have given me these nine cats lives! I pray I will fulfill His purpose despite my physical limitations.

## I'm getting old

*I'm getting old; this outer mortal shell now fails.*
*Lord Jesus draw my restless soul to rest in You.*
*For undiminished sight I sought; that also pales.*
*A fresher sight of You I need, to see me through.*

*I'm getting old; I cannot always clearly hear.*
*But Lord, it is far better still to hear Your voice,*
*To feel Your presence with me and to know You're near.*
*In this most priceless gift of Yours, may I rejoice.*

*I'm getting old; I stumble as I try to walk.*
*But Lord, it is more valuable to walk Your way,*
*To closely walk with You, and with You often talk,*
*Be always under Your Almighty, Holy sway.*

*I'm getting old; my energy has almost gone,*
*But give Your promised strength, that I may serve You still*
*And from my feeble life, Your glorious light be shone.*
*I need Your Holy Spirit, Lord, my life to fill.*

*I'm getting old; my once sharp memory is poor,*
*But may Your precious Words in me not e'er depart.*
*May I still meditate of them yet more and more,*
*Those Living words, each day, You've planted in my heart.*

*I'm getting old; my body often groans with pain,*
*Not taking easily to gradual decline.*
*Lord, help me keep my eyes on You, and not complain.*
*On Your unfailing mercies and Your grace recline.*

*I'm getting old; this fragile transient body's health*
*Is waning in increasing measure, ever fast.*
*But Lord, it's You I have; You are my greatest wealth.*
*So keep me very close, 'till I'm with You at last.*

*I'm getting old; You're drawing me from earthbound things,*
*Removed those things on which I wrongly once relied.*
*But Lord, it is from You I drink those heavenly springs.*
*In awe I fall before Your feet; in You abide.*

# What next?

# CHAPTER 28

"The path of the righteous is like a shining light which shines more and more until the perfect day." Proverbs 4.18

I am nearly eighty years old as I write this; my first and probably my last book. I have just heard on the television news how soon the brain starts to lose some of its function – as early as the mid forties and certainly by the time one is a senior citizen. My experience is rather different, for although my short term memory is poor, my brain seems more active than ever! I am writing many more poems now, some I have included here and which I hope will not have overwhelmed you!

However, it is true, my body is not what it was and I cannot do the things I once did. I cannot go shopping without a wheelchair and I find it hard to even walk around our little cottage. But praise the Lord, I have been lent four wheels and I have a fit, helpful and very loving husband who is willing, not only to push me around town, but also to do the vast majority of jobs in the house. While Tony does practically all the physical work, I have been writing until my hand has nearly fallen off, for we are both computer illiterate! Our roles have thus been reversed, but I rather like it this way and he seems to also!

There is no strong bible believing church near us out in the country, so we took the plunge and joined a Grace Baptist Church eight miles away. However, there were questions I had been asking; "What do You want me to do, Lord? How can I best serve You? What is next on Your agenda for my life in this church? After awhile with virtually nothing emerging, a sense of uselessness began to envelop me. It was not that I felt too old for the Lord to use, but rather that there was little or no outlet for any ministry, apart from playing the piano.

I have developed a kindred spirit with a lady called Ann Clarke at this church. She is totally committed to the Lord and His work all the time, never seems to tire although she is not well and has little or no rest. She is very generous despite possessing little of this worlds goods, and she never talks about herself, only the Lord and what He is teaching her as she pores over the Word of God. Her prayer life is the overflow of a heart filled with Scripture; deeply moving Holy Spirit prayers; for repentance and for revival. Ann is someone who has gone further, more sacrificially up the steep climb which leads to the heavenly summit, and she is stretching out a hand to lift me up in my old age and in my many infirmities. It has usually seemed to have been me helping others spiritually, and so I welcome this provision from the Lord with open arms. At last there is someone outside my family, and near at hand, who cares enough for my soul.

We are from very different backgrounds, Ann coming from the east end of London and yet we have very much in common. Our personalities are quite similar, particularly that we are both really determined characters. We both have a prophetic edge to our ministry – she in our present church and I in the last where Tony and I ministered – so I welcome Ann's calling and applaud her courage. One day in the course of conversation on the phone, Ann picked me up for being too forward in talking to people; too overwhelmingly strong and that I should remember that I was no longer the minister's wife. She told me that people in this church would not be able to cope with a woman like me. I was utterly crushed and for a moment felt like running away, though I never conveyed this to her. It was out of her concern for me that she spoke as she did for she wanted to protect me, but I urged her not to. Then I came across Margaret Barker in our congregation. Not knowing anything about me or Ann's remark, she took me aside one Sunday and said, "I can see you are a minister's wife, for I have noticed the way you go round talking to everyone." My reaction was; "No, no, I am not supposed to be a minister's wife anymore. I won't be accepted here." Margaret looked at me with such compassion and somehow sensing how I felt, said "We want people like you here. We need you. The Lord has given you a wonderful ministry to all kinds of different people." Each time we met in church again, she kept repeating this.

So what then is my *next ministry*? Is there any for a person like me in my old age? Can I still serve the Lord in the church to which I have been called? He has shown me that the answer is indeed yes! There are two particular, behind the scenes ministries, of vital importance, which I

am still able to do for the Lord; one is that of encouragement and exhortation and the other is that of intercession.

## Encouragement

*Encouragement, a mellowed gift.*
*Each situation carefully sift.*
*Ne'er silence quench, where words uplift*
*The fainting heart in manner swift.*

*Encouragement these days is rare.*
*Seen impropriety; a snare*
*To true humility. A prayer*
*Be more appropriate to share!*

*Encouragement that's then withheld*
*Turns cold the heart. Unparalleled*
*The boomerang effect propelled*
*T'wards those who've not this gift upheld.*

*Encouragement fulfills a need*
*For broken hearts, once rent, that bleed.*
*Each one of us this gift should heed,*
*And for its operation plead.*

*Encouragement's personified*
*In Barnabas; exemplified*
*By others too, and typified*
*Through words most apt and well applied.*

*'Encouragement' – through ages rings*
*This clarion call, for joy it brings*
*To saddened hearts; but ever clings*
*To God, the source of all its springs.*

To be an effective encourager, one of the most important virtues needed is humility – a grace for which I constantly pray as I realise my lack; a humility that looks out for others virtues and giftings and then tells them how much they are appreciated, a humility that forgets itself and reaches out to comfort those who are suffering and often silently, a humility that seeks the best for others rather than for itself and will risk reputation to warn and exhort others to repent. "For those that turn many to righteousness are wise and will shine like the stars in the heavens." Daniel 12.3. This Barnabas ministry is a Cinderella, being sadly neglected, and all too rare.

## Humility

*Humility – a grace that's rare.*
*It shows itself in word and deed.*
*For others, more than self will care.*
*A heav'nly, holy grace indeed.*

*Humility will never boast*
*Except in God, its strength and source.*
*It loves to honour others most,*
*And draws its power from God's resource.*

*For powerful is humility*
*To oil the wheels of fractiousness.*
*It calms all rude hostility*
*With peacefulness and lowliness.*

*Humility itself forgets.*
*It's happy never to have been*
*Important; but instead, it lets*
*All other's merits more be seen.*

*Humility is beautiful.*
*I'm such a one who needs this grace.*
*Oh, make my heart so bountiful*
*That true humility embrace.*

If there is anything of any merit recorded here, it is NOT due to anything in me. It has been the Lord's doing, His enabling and His grace. As Paul writes, "What have we that we have not received?" The answer of course is absolutely nothing! It was the Lord's kindness to give me such an exciting and fulfilling life, though hard indeed. To live for Jesus IS the ultimate adventure! My response to Him is profound gratitude.

However, life has not finished yet; not only have I been blessed in the past, but I am still being blessed in countless ways, and furthermore I have an even brighter future ahead. How can I possibly know this? It is because I believe the Bible, and Proverbs 4.18 assures me that "The path of the righteous is like a shining light that shines more and more until the perfect day."

## The best is still to come

*If I had still my health as in past years,*
*How very different would my life now be.*
*I might some days spend time in many spheres*
*Which in imagination only see.*

*Walking in bluebell woods, I could be free*
*To catch the beauty of the carpet's hue,*
*Stretching sometimes as far as eye can see;*
*A springtime glory, a splendiferous view.*

*Surfing excitedly, as rolling wave*
*Propels me forward fast upon its course,*
*A ride which cost is only to be brave,*
*Because the mighty sea has mighty force.*

*Travelling abroad to yonder distant shore;*
*New sights to see, exotic foods to taste.*
*Mysterious ancient monuments explore.*
*This special opportunity not waste.*

*Climbing hills, with panoramic vista*
*Spread before the eyes, and fresh mountain air*
*That fills the breast with life's sweet lustre,*
*And causes all to gasp, and stand, and stare.*

*So many different things I once could do.*
*But looking back, with gratitude for all*
*Past memories, I know there's something new*
*To grasp – the poignancy of God's clear call.*

He tells us that the best is yet to come.
The path before us is a shining light,
Which shines the more, until it will become
The perfect day, that shines in glory bright.

The visits to the hospitals become
The outings of such opportunity.
Each one adventure filled, as with someone
We share the gospel, in simplicity.

God uses all frustrations, weakness, pain,
To teach us patience; Him to emulate.
And as we look to Him, we find we gain
New vision, to enhance, invigorate.

The simple things of life are beautified;
They amply satisfy the heav'n-bound soul.
The blessings of God's Word are multiplied;
They fill the place that earthly things once stole.

We learn to feel the pain of others more.
We enter in, where angels fear to tread,
Hear treasured secrets, in our hearts to store
For prayer, which has become our life's main thread.

God teaches us to wait on Him, be still.
He draws us close; the world is left behind.
There is no loss, but only space to fill
For Him who is so wonderfully kind.

*No fear of want, or desperate need we see.*
*To live is Jesus Christ; to die is gain.*
*It is in Him we live, to Him we flee.*
*We long for Jesus in our lives to reign.*

*So, both looking back and looking forward*
*We well can see how truly blessed we are.*
*For we're bound to travelling ever shoreward,*
*Till we meet our SAVIOUR; the Morning Star.*

Years ago I met a girl of about nine, called Katie. Later I heard that she had cancer of the brain which she fought bravely for years. A month ago, when she had now turned twenty six, another quite different form of cancer developed in her brain and this one was even more aggressive. I heard that she had only a very short time to live and that all who knew her were challenged by her holiness, her love of Jesus and her longing to be with Him in heaven. So I decided to write her a letter in poetry form and here it is.

## A letter to brave Katie

*I once remember meeting you,*
*And looking back I'm proud.*
*You were a girl that many knew,*
*Just one among a crowd.*

*But now that you've become a star,*
*Your story I will tell,*
*For this has got enormous power*
*The greatest fear to quell.*

*I wonder who has ever heard*
*A story like this one?*
*A life so young, yet undeterred,*
*By illness overrun.*

*It started when she was a child.*
*It started in her brain.*
*The doctors knew it was not mild,*
*But ne'er did she complain.*

*She's grown into a woman now,*
*And what a woman too!*
*All those who know her, wonder how*
*She's coped these long years through.*

*She's talented at poetry*
*And art and music too.*
*Remembered for posterity,*
*By those she never knew.*

*But more than this, by greater far*
*Is beauty that's within.*
*No sickness, pain, can ever mar*
*The grace that's placed therein.*

*For this is not a story*
*In usual story books,*
*But one that gives the glory*
*To One to whom she looks.*

*he is a challenge to us all*
*To fix our eyes on Him,*
*And daily, hourly, on Him call,*
*Like her, a cherubim.*

*I've rarely heard of anyone*
*So ill, yet free from fears,*
*Because her heart to heaven's been won,*
*And this has brought me tears.*

*Tears of joy this saint has brought me.*
*For she loves her Lord so much*
*That most she longs her Lord to see*
*And Him in heaven touch.*

*I pray that those in deep distress*
*Will trust the Lord she knows*
*And through her witness many bless,*
*With victory that she shows.*

*Her story will go round the world*
*One day, I am assured.*
*The banner of her Lord unfurled*
*In suffering well endured.*

*So nothing's wasted, nothings lost*
*With life so short, so blessed.*
*It has fulfilled, though at great cost,*
*His purpose and His best.*

I received a reply by return of post and this is what she wrote. "Dear Gillian, Thank you so much for sending me the truly beautiful poem 'To brave Katie.' I don't feel brave very often, but it is really incredible what God has done and is doing. I don't know how He does it, but that's part of the mystery!! If I did know I would be bigger than Him, and I much prefer having Him bigger than me! … I am so looking forward to walking through the door called 'death' and living forever in the house of God! I'll see you there later! Lots of love, Katie. xxx."

You can imagine the huge impact this had on me she had so decreased that He had increased. Since starting this chapter and very soon after receiving her letter, dear Katie has gone to be with her Lord. Five hundred people crowded the church in Birmingham, for five hundred and probably many more, knew how special she was and how she had blazed the trail for them at such a young age. Katie obviously knew, beyond a shadow of doubt, that the best was still to come or she could not have written such a letter. She was even longing to go through the door of death. Why? Surely it was because she knew the Saviour well enough and the Scriptures well enough, particularly the book of Revelation, that she was able joyfully to anticipate the wonders of what was soon to become her heavenly home.

So then, what is my *next destination?* It is surely heaven too. Like Katie, I have read Revelation many times, absorbed much of its contents and am revelling in its promises with increasing amazement. Just think what our future will be if we are washed in the blood of the Lamb, sealed and truly the redeemed of the Lord. We will be set free from all the limitations, frustrations and problems of this life. There will be no more pain, no hunger, no thirst, no tears, no sorrow, no night, no death and no curse.

We shall experience wonderful new things. We shall **hear** sounds more beautiful than ever imagined. There will be the 'songs of Moses and the Lamb,' new songs that angels sing, many different instruments playing, the praises of all God's people, and above all the great voice of Jesus which is like the sound of many waters. We shall **see** sights that will enthral us; there in heaven will be all the redeemed in white, who feared God, gave Him glory and overcame the devil. We will see the beauty of heaven's jewels, its golden streets and the pure crystal river of life proceeding from the throne and from the Lamb. Above all; we shall see Jesus on the throne surrounded by the rainbow, the great Lion of Judah, yet with clothing dipped in blood. His name will be written on His thigh, KING OF KINGS AND LORD OF LORDS. His head once crowned with thorns, will be crowned with many crowns, and more wonderful still, we shall see His face, the face that was so marred, but now resplendent in all its beauty.

We shall not be idle, but **doing** many things; celebrating the marriage supper of the Lamb, serving God day and night, worshipping Him with all the angels, meeting all those multitudes standing before the throne, praising Him and giving Him glory and honour and power. And we shall be led to those living waters from which we may freely drink. What great delights and what joy will be ours! How thankful we will be that we have His Name on our foreheads. How relieved that we have been given the right to the tree of life. The newness of heaven and the holiness of this city under His holy reign will utterly surpass our wildest dreams.

Heaven is what I am preparing for and that for which I long. Heaven is being in the presence of His glory, unhindered by every earthly obstacle. I earnestly pray that while here on earth, my greatest delight, continual choice and more constant experience will be to walk in the light of His presence unhindered by the sins that still so easily beset me. For it is only then that His Shekinah glory will be manifested in my life and so draw others to Him.

## Your presence

*Your presence Lord is what I yearn*
*With ever trembling heart.*
*Teach me, that I at last may learn*
*The secret of my part.*

*To know You more and more I long,*
*With lowliness of mind.*
*Lift me above the worldly throng,*
*Your character to find.*

*To hear You speak in clear still voice,*
*The sweetest that I know,*
*Has caused me greatly to rejoice,*
*In praise to overflow.*

*To sense You're here, to feel Your touch*
*Brings comfort to my heart.*
*May I, from now, love You so much*
*That ne'er from You depart.*

*To see Your glory, Lord, I ask.*
*To worship at your feet.*
*And in Your presence Lord to bask*
*Is surely joy complete.*

*Your presence Lord is all I need*
*Each moment of the day.*
*Your presence Lord is what I plead,*
*So keep me close I pray.*

Recently a couple called Sue and John Willington, who are relatively new Christians, asked me if they could take my large cross to use for evangelism amongst the down and outs, drug addicts and alcoholics on the streets. Of course I agreed and they came to collect it and spent two hours with us, during which time I was challenged to the core. Here were people not speaking my *spiritual* language, but with a depth of knowledge of the Father's love, a heart and a life to reach the lost, a humility to accept correction immediately, a joy bursting from their innermost being shining radiantly in their faces and a passion for Jesus Christ that vastly outstripped mine. It made me hang my head in shame, but also spurred me on to realise something more of the implications the cross should have in my life. It should more thoroughly permeate my whole being, so that I am crossed out and Jesus alone is exalted.

Thus I am discovering, increasingly, how much more 'land there is still to be possessed.' So I echo the words of St. Paul in Phil 3.14 and 10; "One thing I do, I press towards the mark for the prize of the high calling of God in Christ Jesus" … This then is my ONE GOAL that "I may know Him, the power of His resurrection and the fellowship of His sufferings, being conformed to His death." I pray that in this way I may endeavour with all earnestness to make Jesus known, *whatever the cost*, until that awesome day when I shall see Him face to face. Amen.

## St. John's vision of Jesus

*O Son of man, clothed with a garment bright*
*Down to the feet; the chest with golden band*
*And head of hair like snow; a wondrous sight,*
*Soft eyes aflame with fire of love You stand.*

*Your feet of brass refined in furnace hot,*
*And hotter than a man has ever dreamt,*
*Yet voice so sweet and flawless, without spot,*
*The sound of many waters, floods pre-empt.*

*You have the golden stars in Your right hand,*
*And from Your mouth goes out a two-edged sword.*
*Your glorious countenance makes sun seem bland,*
*Shining in strength; yes now must all applaud.*

*You are the One who died; the crucified,*
*Yet are alive, alive for evermore.*
*You have the keys of death and hell; decide*
*Who enters heaven's gate; from time foresaw.*

*The Alpha and Omega soon draws near.*
*He is coming back, and every eye shall see*
*The glorious Son of God in clouds appear,*
*The One we pierced and nailed to cruel tree.*

*He is coming soon for those washed in His blood,*
*From satan's grip and sinner's lifestyle torn.*
*Washed clean as snow by fountains crimson flood,*
*While others sigh and weep and watch and mourn.*

*But when I see Him there, fall down I will,*
*And worship at His feet, and kiss His head.*
*My tears of sorrow, joy and love, will spill*
*Upon the One whose blood for me was shed.*

Revelation 1. 4–8 & 13–18

To contact Gillian go to Facebook page
'One Goal whatever the cost'
and send her a message.